THINKING CHRISTIANLY

CHRISTIAN HIGHER EDUCATION AND A VIGOROUS LIFE OF THE MIND

Essays In Memory of Thomas E. Corts

Edited by Paul R. Corts

Sherman Oak Books
Samford University Press
Birmingham, Alabama

Sherman Oak Books of
Samford University Press

Samford University
800 Lakeshore Drive
Birmingham, Alabama 35229, U.S.A.
www.samford.edu
©2011 by Samford University Press

ISBN 978-1-931985-18-9

Cataloging-in-Publication Data available
from the Library of Congress

Printed and bound in the
United States of America

DEDICATION

In memory of Tom Corts's extraordinary loyalty
to his parents and siblings for the impact
they had on shaping his character and life,
this book is dedicated to them.

In memory of Charles Harold Corts – Father
In memory of Hazel Louise Vernon Corts – Mother
Naomi Ruth White – Sister
John Ronald Corts – Brother
In memory of Charles Mark Corts – Brother
David Livingston Corts – Brother
Paul Richard Corts – Brother
In memory of Philip Chris Corts – Brother

THINKING CHRISTIANLY:

CHRISTIAN HIGHER EDUCATION AND A VIGOROUS LIFE OF THE MIND

Essays In Memory of Thomas E. Corts

Edited by Paul R. Corts

Contents

Acknowledgements

This gedenkschrift for Thomas E. Corts required
the collaboration and kindness of a host of individuals.
My task as editor was made much easier because of the
reservoir of goodwill accumulated by my brother Tom
during his lifetime, but that makes me no less grateful for
the countless ways that so many were helpful in assisting
with the project. I especially appreciate the commitment
of the contributing authors, each a truly exceptional
individual, who provided thoughtful essays that honor
Tom.

My brother was blessed to have married his high
school sweetheart, Marla Haas, who complemented
Tom well, who so loyally walked with him through the
journey of life, and who has been exceptionally helpful
in responding to the plethora of questions I posed to her
throughout this process. I know that Marla also consulted
their children, Jennifer, Rachel, and Chris, and I am
grateful for all of their support for this book.

When the idea for this gedenkschrift was
developing in my mind, I consulted a number of
individuals who affirmed the project and were a source
of encouragement throughout the process. Katy, Paul,

and Shirley Piper, dear friends to Tom and me, were immediately enthusiastic about the project and pledged their financial help for the book. Joe Lewis, a long time friend and colleague of Tom's from his Georgetown College days who later served with Tom at Samford University, committed to help with the myriad of administrative details that would be involved in such an undertaking. Joe gave selflessly, repeatedly, and tirelessly time after time over the year and a half this book has been in process. He represents the kind of friend we all hope to have. Incredibly faithful and loyal to Tom in life, Joe likewise was there whenever I needed him in preparing this memorial volume.

Dr. Andrew Westmoreland, current president of Samford University who immediately succeeded Tom, has been an enthusiastic cheerleader for this project. Andy graciously made available the former and current staff in the president's office to assist – a special thanks to Rebecca Williamson and Sandra O'Brien. Caroline Summers, senior photographer at Samford, was a wonderful help collecting photos for inclusion in the book.

Several of my staff colleagues at the Council for Christian Colleges & Universities (CCCU) have supported me throughout this project and to them I owe special thanks as well, including Jennifer Byrnes, Nate Mouttet, Kyle Royer, Susan Kish, and Kevin Zwirble.

Good friends and leaders of Christian higher education, who have been board chairpersons on the CCCU board during my presidency, have been a source of encouragement to me by making provision for me to be engaged in projects like this on behalf of Christian higher education. I am especially grateful to David Dockery, Bob Brower, Carl Zylstra, and Kim Phipps.

I have been blessed with the good editorial

assistance of Karen Hutto and Ashley Walters. Karen worked with each of the essays to help put them together as a collective whole that reflected unity and coherence. She was a gracious colleague who provided unbiased third party counsel as I bombarded her with innumerable questions. She researched numerous details and assisted in fine-tuning the essays. Ashley, always kind and helpful, interrupted other work to give the entire manuscript a careful final review. Thanks also to Glenn Chandler of Lickwid Design for his expert design skills in designing both the book and the dust jacket.

On countless occasions late at night, early in the morning, on weekends or whenever, my wife Diane has been there to provide answers, counsel, and encouragement to help me see the project through to completion. She endured hearing my frustrations. She politely avoided complaining when her engrossed husband was non-responsive to questions or conversation. She kept dinner warm when I had one more thing I just had to get done before stopping. She willingly missed activities we otherwise would have enjoyed while I labored to accomplish one of the many urgent project demands in a timely fashion. I am truly blessed with a good and godly companion; thank you, Diane.

For all the good this book contains, I thank all those who made it happen. My faith has been buoyed by the countless good deeds and untold kindnesses you have showered on me in this process.

Paul R. Corts
Washington, DC
August 15, 2011

FOREWORD

My brother Tom was a quintessential Christian intellectual. He sought God intensely, loved Christ resolutely, and walked with the Holy Spirit devotedly. He kept the words of a prayer by a medieval bishop in a prominent personal space so that he would be consistently reminded, "Day by day, dear Lord, of thee three things I pray: to see thee more clearly, love thee more dearly, follow thee more nearly, day by day" (Attributed to Richard of Chichester, 1197-1253).

Tom was the fifth-born in a family of seven children, approximately two years separating each. I was born next and became his younger brother, a term of endearment that I have enjoyed through life. He was my brother, but for me he was also "a friend who sticks closer than a brother" (Proverbs 18:24b). While we were not birth twins, throughout our adult lives we were mates. When Tom died, it felt like a part of me died, too.

In the days following the shock of the news of his death, I became gripped with the idea of publishing a collection of essays in book form as an appropriate way to memorialize Tom's life. He was a man of books, and he collected them voraciously. As his family moved into larger homes over the years, larger library spaces were always created for Tom, only to find that the newly enlarged spaces quickly became overflowing with the addition of still more books. A student of antiquity from his study of classical rhetoric, Tom was mesmerized by leather-bound volumes. He would pay dearly for a well-used book, especially one that showed it had been loved with tender care. He was especially fascinated with fore-edge books. Over the years, he collected an assortment of book restoration tools and materials that enabled him to lovingly nurture old volumes to new life, preserving the old for future generations.

Tom's devotion to Christian higher education sprang deep from that same well of desire, preserving the timeless truths of the Christian faith for future generations by helping students engage these institutions' tools, people, curriculum, facilities, and experiences to form a new life of the mind in Christ. Devoted to the highest levels of quality as the only suitable offering to God, he displayed relentless passion to detail and provided the university community with the optimum resources to develop the capacity to think Christianly.

When I shared the vision for this memorial volume with several friends and family members, without exception the responses were unanimous in attesting to the appropriateness of a book to honor Tom's life. Dear friends, the Piper family, agreed to support the project financially. Dr. Andrew Westmoreland, president of Samford University, enthusiastically gave his blessing and unreserved support. Scholars, writers, pastors, and friends – all with varying connections to Tom – were invited to submit essays on the general theme of Christian higher education and the life of the mind in Christ. The many authors who accepted the invitation and whose essays are incorporated in this volume have honored Tom with their contributions to form an eclectic collection.

My prayer, and I believe it would be Tom's as well, is that this volume would be a testimonial of gratitude to the countless numbers of committed Christians through the ages who have nurtured the life of the mind through a life of service in Christian higher education. May it be an inspiration to all who choose vocations of service in Christian higher education in order to encourage future generations to think Christianly.

- *Paul R. Corts*

Editor's Note:

I first met John Stott through worshipping at All Souls Church, Langham Place, off Oxford Circus in Central London, early in my professional career while I was frequenting London to research at the British Public Records Office and the great British libraries for my dissertation on Queen Elizabeth I. Stott was experiencing a meteoric rise within world evangelicalism; and my brother Tom and I, both in the process of becoming Anglophiles, traveled to London regularly, establishing and operating student study programs there. All Souls Church was our house of worship when in London, and we both greatly appreciated Stott as an unapologetic evangelical, championing the intellectual life and the importance of loving God with all our minds. Through a dear mutual friend, Martha Ashe, I later had opportunities to converse and spend time with Stott, and my admiration for his keen intellect grew. I was delighted that Stott graciously offered these words for publication in this book. They are excerpted from a speech he gave to leaders at the London Institute for Contemporary Christianity in 2001.

PREFACE

LIVING THE CHRISTIAN LIFE: THE INEVITABILITY OF THE CONSCIENTIOUS USE OF THE MIND

By John R.W. Stott

It was in my attempt some years ago to combat the spirit of anti-intellectualism (that I still believe is such a bane on the Christian church today), that I dared say for the first time, though I have said it often since, that anti-intellectualism and the fullness of the Holy Spirit are mutually incompatible. And I dared to say it because the Holy Spirit is the spirit of truth. Jesus, our Lord Himself, referred to the Holy Spirit as the spirit of truth, and therefore it is only logical to say that wherever the Holy Spirit is given His freedom, truth is bound to matter. So, I have argued, and argue still, that a proper, conscientious use of our minds is an inevitable part and parcel of our Christian life.

Firstly, a proper use of our minds glorifies our Creator. We believe that He is a rational God who has made us in His own image and likeness, rational men and women. And He has given us a rational revelation of Himself.

Secondly, a proper use of the mind enriches our Christian discipleship. There is no aspect of our discipleship that can be developed without the use of our mind. Whatever part of discipleship you are reflecting on – worship, faith, guidance – the mind has an indispensable part to play.

Thirdly, a proper use of the mind strengthens our witness in the world. I am still convinced that one of the major reasons why people reject the gospel in the West today is not because they perceive it to be false, but because they perceive it to be trivial. They think it is inadequate for the complexities and challenges of the world today. We know of course that in evangelism, in conversion and regeneration, the Holy Spirit, again, has an indispensable part to play. Only He can lead a sinner to Christ. But when He leads us to Christ, He does not do it in spite of the evidence, but because of the evidence when He opens our minds to attend to it.

So to sum up, anti-intellectualism insults God, impoverishes us, and weakens our testimony in the world. In contrast, a proper use of the mind glorifies God, enriches us, and strengthens our witness in the world.

Thinking Christianly

Christian Higher Education and a Vigorous Life of the Mind

Essays In Memory of Thomas E. Corts

Edited by Paul R. Corts

Editor's Note:

Tom first met Bill Hull in the fall of 1964 when he attended Southern Baptist Theological Seminary for a semester. Dr. Hull taught his New Testament Survey course. After Tom became Samford University's president, the provost retired, opening the position. Tom drove to Shreveport where Hull was serving as a pastor to discuss the provost position with him. To avoid speculation that might come from dining publicly, Bill's wife Wylodine prepared dinner for them, and they dined in the Hull home. Hull accepted Tom's invitation to become provost and served with distinction from 1987-1996, when he retired. From my conversations with both, I know the two men mutually shared enormous personal, intellectual, and spiritual respect. I thought Hull's eulogy at the memorial service for Tom would serve as a perfect introduction to this book.

INTRODUCTION

PUBLIC REFLECTIONS ON A PRIVATE PERSON

By William E. Hull

To understand the spirituality of Tom Corts, we must first explore why it is often said that he was a private person. Although he was open and accessible to his many constituencies, he never sought shallow relationships by working a crowd in backslapping fashion. Although he made many acquaintances, he had few close friends, particularly at work where cronyism can undermine a sense of fairness in the distribution of rewards. Although he adored his wife, he did not demonstrate that affection by embracing or kissing her in public, reserving such intimacies for a tight family circle seldom on display. Although he was a deeply religious person, he refrained from using a lot of God-talk or leading a season of prayer every time he was confronted with a problem.

One always had the sense that there was more to Tom than met the eye; that he had a sort of secret self, a hidden dimension, a hinterland of mystery where it would be inappropriate to intrude. It was not that he wished to conceal himself from those who wanted to know him better. Rather, he seemed to view this private domain as a holy of holies that was not his to control because it belonged, not to him, but to God.

In his 1843 book, *Fear and Trembling*, the Danish philosopher Søren Kierkegaard described "the Knight of Faith," which offers us a classic exploration of Tom's inner sanctum.[1] When self is replaced by God at the core of one's being, it is no longer necessary to parade one's deepest commitments in outward fashion because now, whatever one does, whether at work or at play, is an expression of that inwardness. Just as self-centeredness finally permeates everything one thinks and feels and decides, so Tom's God-centeredness enabled him to live his entire life in harmony with what Kierkegaard called "the movements of infinity," or Pascal called "the motions of grace." Let us notice three ways that this private spirituality shaped his public responsibilities.

First, Tom lived a self-examined life. Alfred North Whitehead famously remarked that religion is what one does with one's solitude. Tom used that brooding silence to listen for a still small voice often lost in the noisy public square. He engaged in rigorous introspection lest his motives become corrupted by external pressures. He read Scripture carefully, prayed earnestly, and journaled faithfully to refresh the wellsprings of his spiritual vitality. Because he determined to live life from the inside out rather than from the outside in, he knew that nothing else would be right unless he was right with God in that lonely encounter, where he could bring no one but himself.

Second, Tom sequestered his faith to protect it from the pressures of a socially contrived consensus. The mass media has become so powerful and pervasive that it can crystallize public opinion almost overnight. Only those leaders who hold themselves apart from the current craze for connectivity remain free to find their way beyond it. Whether restating a charter or revising a constitution, Tom felt unafraid to challenge the status quo because his conscience was not captive to the latest poll.

Third, this practice of inwardness was not based on a disdain for others but rather a desire to help them. So many leaders today seem to draw their strength from the celebrity culture. They want to bask in the spotlight, to appear on the best talk shows, to exult in the frenzy of renown. Soon they find themselves doing whatever it takes to maintain that lofty perch, squandering their hard-earned reputations with endless compromise. By contrast, Tom did not draw power from the people but gave power to the people from his well-stocked mind, his sensitive conscience, and his passion for human betterment. As Emerson once put it, "The saint and the poet seek privacy to ends the most public and universal." [2]

We live in a day when religion has become militantly aggressive: In your face; wear it on your sleeve so nobody can miss where you stand; put it in the U. S. Constitution; pass laws to enforce its precepts; play politics to gain the backing of government for its agenda. But we gather here to honor a man who did just the opposite. He practiced his religion in private because he had learned from his Master that the secret of religion is that religion is secret (Matthew 6:1-18). This modesty never muted his witness, however, because he lived out his faith in everything he did.

Thus his example leaves each one of us with a question. If we could not make a single religious claim but had to depend entirely on the evidence of the life we live, would others know where we stand regarding the ultimate issues of life?

Dr. Hull's eulogy was originally presented at the memorial service for Thomas Edward Corts, held at the Wright Center, Samford University, Birmingham, Alabama, on February 8, 2009.

References:

1. Robert Bretall, ed., *A Kierkegaard Anthology* (Princeton: Princeton University Press, 1951), 118-29.

2. Cited by William Deresiewicz, "The End of Solitude," *Chronicle of Higher Education* (January 30, 2009), B7.

Editor's Note:

My brother Tom and I talked to each other regularly. There were few major decisions either of us made without first talking with the other. We also shared deep conversations about our faith and our work in Christian higher education. Tom chose to be a Southern Baptist as a young adult for a variety of reasons, but the Southern Baptist commitment to be evangelical and to stress education were important factors in his decision. He gave his life to the work of Christian higher education. At the capstone of his career, Tom delivered the H. I. Hester Lecture to his lifelong colleagues during the annual meeting of the Association of Southern Baptist Colleges and Schools, held May 31-June 2, 2004, in Franklin, Tennessee. In many ways, his views in this lecture represent a thoughtful coalescence of his experiences, feelings, and beliefs from his life of servant leadership in Christian higher education, and it is altogether fitting for this lecture to serve as the first chapter of this book.

CHAPTER 1

THE UNIVERSITY, THE CHURCH, AND THE CULTURE

By Thomas E. Corts

The New Testament concept of being "in this world, but not of this world," summarizes the dilemma of each of us, personally, and of our institutions.[1] The church (in this paper, I shall use "the church" as representing the great body of all Christian believers), and especially Evangelicals in America, has alternately "struggled with an inherent tension between... keeping that which they defined as sacred uncontaminated by the profane world" and "infusing the world with sanctifying influences."[2] In other words, should we keep separate and apart from the world or become involved in the world in order to win the world for Christ? From the first century A.D., and even under the Emperor Constantine and in the Dark Ages, there has been an uneasy coexistence between culture and Christianity – Caesar and Christ, *paideia* and *Logos*.[3]

Now by culture, I mean the totality of socially transmitted behavior patterns, art, science, beliefs, and all products of human work and thought, the collected wisdom and sentiment of past and present.[4] In America especially, our culture and our Christianity have been at times friends, and at times, enemies. Yet, speaking in frank generalities, it is probably true today that modern American culture has overwhelmed modern American Christianity.[5] The ceaseless waves of messages from movies, newspapers, TV, have acculturated a sea of secularism and spawned a rip-tide, pulling American Christians under. At the risk of gross oversimplification, it seems that with deliberate speed in the post-World War II era, prosperity came to great numbers in this country, allowing the rising middle class Christian masses to imbibe the consumerist pop culture until bloated and tranquilized by the transitory sweetness of the good life to sink into the sea of cultural abyss.

The editor of *Christian Century* said in 1948 that three separate forces were bidding for ascendancy in the spiritual life of America: Protestantism, Roman Catholicism, and secularism.[6] As we look back on the fifty years from 1950 to 2000, a time of radically shifting realities, secularism has won thus far. Consider what happened in that approximate time frame. Virtually everyone with half an inclination and minimal preparation was able to go to high school and on to college. Marriage and the family came under harsh attack. Birth control made women freer. Sex was lifted from its undercover status in public conversation. Rebellion and civil disobedience became more acceptable.

We confronted racial prejudice and outlawed segregation. Laws made work less offensive and demanding. Easy credit taught us not to defer our desires, but to have it all without waiting. Clothing styles and dress codes lost their modesty. Relentlessly catchy slogans and rhythms stuck in our brains so that we repeated advertising without conscious intent. Urban so-called music, with ribald language, demeaning to women and flaunting street vernacular's dirtiest words, tumbled from the lips of mere kiddies, *sans* anything harmonious. Holding to freedoms that the Founding Fathers likely never would have allowed, we endured the outrageous – the truly uncouth outrageous – on TV halftime shows, on commercials, on billboards, and in other public venues, stretching the bounds of public taste. We not only *tolerated* the cult of personality among stars of athletics, movies, TV, and public prominence, we *made* those stars, sometimes even allowing them to invent themselves and rewarding them with obscene profits as compensation for their illicit theft of the unmerited admiration of our young. [7]

And what of the church? I wish I could say, "Praise the Lord! The church has stood firm, unmovable against the cultural trash that least admirably represents our national scene." But, sadly, I cannot. I had hoped that the billions we have spent on Sunday schools, day schools, and vacation Bible schools would produce a generation that has its values correct.[8] I would have thought the vast sums spent on television preaching might have turned the tide.

I wish all the church buildings and all the churchgoing had made a consistent and measurable difference. But we are left to admit: the divorce rate is about the same among those who attend church and those who do not. The 70 percent of men between the ages of eighteen and thirty-four who visit a pornography website at least once a month includes believers and church-goers.[9] The ranks of the high-and-mighty white-collar elite who have bilked us for billions includes those Bible-carrying, church-going, God-talking criminals who will escape jail, only by legal sleight-of-hand if they do escape.[10] As the Barna Organization has concluded, "Peoples' faith does not make as much of a difference as might be expected . . . ."[11]

The Effects of Today's Torrent of Information

Now having already made so many strong statements, it is probably time for a disclaimer. In this generation it is the privilege of the old to condemn the young. It is probably characteristic that every reigning class of senior citizens thinks theirs was the greatest generation and that whatever comes along afterward will not be as good. In the interest of full disclosure, I herewith admit to being a card-carrying member of AARP, to being granted the senior citizen discount at a fast food restaurant, even without confessing my age. While my intent here is to be objective and fair, you can now beware.

I was a lowly graduate student when I first read a book by anthropologist Edward T. Hall, *The Silent Language*.[12] Hall's idea is that communication is far more than what we *say*; it encompasses non-verbal communication and the sum total of our actions and behavior. A subtle, subconscious patterning of conduct and behavior results from communication gathered into what we come to know as culture. In *sub rosa* ways we never recognize these collective communications, woven into the warp and woof of our culture, become the ever-so-silently conveyed meanings that influence our attitudes, that plant ideas, reinforce positions, fashion our taste and sense of propriety, cultivate familiarity – all by stealth.[13] We have more means of messaging – they come at us faster than any other civilization in history – and from this torrent of communication, culture is going to be formed, modified, adapted, and with greater alacrity than ever before, even as other elements of culture will be more readily rejected, forgotten, shunted aside. This cheap, easy, and almost continuous communication intensifies the impact of culture.

For instance, our students' lives will be shaped by cell phones and email, the ease with which they can communicate anywhere, any time. They all have calling plans that access the world and preprogrammed country codes to talk with friends in the military on aircraft carriers thousands of miles away and to mission volunteers on other continents. In 1950, about a million overseas phone calls originated in the U.S. In 2001, the number was a staggering 6.27 billion.[14] Email messages float in cyberspace with unimaginable ease and cheapness, among the four billion existing websites, with tens of thousands being added daily.[15] The computer and website are fast becoming teenagers' favorite source for entertainment.[16] Those email messages and chat rooms, for good and for ill, affect our culture, uniting friends and families, accounting for billions of dollars of sales, provoking marriage and divorce, sharing information that resolves problems and heals disease, facilitating crime and mischief, and coordinating terrorist acts anywhere on earth.

All this communication capacity means news spreads rapidly and by multiple means, releasing gigabytes of information to impact our culture, which in turn, impacts each of us. (For example, Samford University had 185,000 Internet hits in the month of April.) The capacity for names and new words to appear suddenly in everyday usage is astounding. Terms like "24/7," "text messaging," and "googling" have come from cyberspace to achieve practical usage.[17] Politicians have known for years that name recognition is crucial. That is why yard signs, billboards, and TV commercials become so important to candidates. In the voting booth, if a voter has no strong conviction, he tends to pull the lever beside the name that seems most familiar – despite whether he knows anything about the individual.

Now, as media within our culture regularly discuss divorce, adultery, murder, racial strife, and homosexuality, we are being conditioned. The terms become more acceptable, more a part of our subconscious, almost routine. That is true, also, of curses, and the four-letter words of movies and rap music, so offensive to my generation. They have become matter-of-fact to our children and grandchildren so that they have lost their shock value. Their frequent use breeds familiarity, in the same sense that brand names become ensconced in our memories and repetition fastens candidates' names on the memory hook of our awareness.

Perhaps this subtle cultural influence can be seen more clearly by looking at a foreign country, where acquaintance with America is quite limited. In Damascus, Syria, the TV series *Seinfeld* airs twice daily. For many young Syrians watching American programs affords them a chance to practice their English. What will a young Syrian conclude about American culture on the basis of *Seinfeld?* Similarly, a Syrian teacher of English asks plaintively for help in explaining American family life to her students. She asks, "Does *Friends* show a typical family?" To the Arab world, this is the insight we currently provide to our Christian culture.[18]

Clearly, the fourth estate, the public media, play a huge role. It was reported a few years ago that the average person processes at least 500 distinct messages per day through sensory perception. With the advent of email, fax, cell phones, text-messaging, etc., it surely must be at least double that number. The news buffet served to us daily by the media tends never to involve the routine or the normal. It almost always relates some extreme or exceptional human behavior. News professionals admit their inclination to feature what is unusual. "Dog bites man" is not newsworthy. "Man bites dog" is. And add to that the fact that our culture influences even the choices the media make. So, if the culture seems inordinately interested in sex, or in children, pets, or whatever, even the media's judgment about what to feature will be tainted by the culture.

When a deranged mother is accused of murdering her children, the story leads, even if she is miles away and obviously very ill. A basketball star is charged with rape. An adult teacher has children with one of her students. A child, barely a teenager, is kidnapped by a strange polygamist who plans to make her his wife.[19] Sexual-related torment of prisoners by guards at the Abu Ghraib prison in Iraq ran among the lead stories for eighteen straight days, and is not over yet. These are all stories that have fascinated the public and have occupied our air waves – not just with one-shot, thirty-second spots, but in an ongoing way, tying up the lead story position for days, and reflected in TV, magazines, and newspapers, all looking for exclusive angles.

Now, my point is that our culture's seductive pull is strengthened by making evil interesting – far more interesting to most than good. There would have been nothing newsworthy, if, like the average household in America, that mother had given her children lunch, seen them to soccer practice, piano lessons, etc. The basketball star's visit to a Colorado resort would not have attracted attention. If an adult teacher taught her schoolchildren and went home to her family, why would media notice? Had the polygamist merely proposed to an Oregon teenager, it would have been rebuffed as insignificant and gone unreported. Holding prisoners in a Baghdad prison is expected and not the stuff of breaking news. In each of these cases, it was the evil, the wrong, that made the situation exceptional, and it was the evil that made purveyors of news confident of the public's interest.

What happens, when news of aberrant behavior is spread in headlines, photographs, newsreel footage, and repeated over and again? Repetition is one of the great learning devices and that wrongful conduct is planted in the mind. Unintentionally, evil is being advertised in prime media space, with the utmost emphasis, so that the masses cannot avoid it. Such advertising costs commercial corporations huge sums of money, yet evil is granted this prime play *au gratis*. And worse, evil even gets favored positioning that no ad agency in America can obtain for its client at any price: the top right hand corner of the daily newspaper; the lead story on the ten o'clock news; and continuous play as emerging details enhance the story.

So, we are victimized by the culture in a vicious cycle. Public taste seeks stories of deviant behavior, of persons with evil intent. The media give the people the stories of evil in the world, and the repetition of the accounts of evil make us all more at ease, more comfortable, less likely to object to stories of evil. Evil enjoys a heyday.

You are familiar with *The Screwtape Letters*. With apologies to the memory of C. S. Lewis, I have this vision of Screwtape writing Wormwood, something like the following:

My Dear Wormwood,

Congratulations are in order. I must say you are working well with clothing designers, actors and actresses, moviemakers, sports stars, media outlets, and people who influence public taste. They are beginning to enjoy a little good old-fashioned lust. We could not be getting better publicity. Our side is well represented in the best newspapers, TV, movies, and in all the media.

And we are reaching the young who have the rest of their lives before them. Every adolescent schoolgirl is striving to be sexy and seductive. In fairly short time, we have engineered a massive increase in the permissiveness society allows. Here and there one hears objections, but children have to learn that sexual expression is healthy, and they are going to know the facts of life sooner or later. It thrills me that people are not hearing all that virtuous pap; instead, every day they become more familiar with the naturalness of hatred, lying, adultery, and promiscuity.

As you know, we must be unrelenting in wearing down the objections of the Enemy. Greed, lust, enmity – people have to realize that these are just human realities. If you can keep it up, dear Nephew, evil will be better known than Coca-Cola, people will no longer mouth all that religious stuff,

*unhappiness will be long-lasting, and we will
have achieved success.*

Your affectionate uncle,

SCREWTAPE

(Adapted after the style of C. S. Lewis, The
Screwtape Letters, *1961.)*

The Gradual Impact of the Cultural Shift

None of us single-handedly chose this culture that
spreads evil more readily than virtue. Yet it is the culture in
which we do our work, the culture in which our lives are
lived, and in which our institutions will falter or prosper.
It is the culture of the people we serve.[20] Perhaps it is true,
that as the social authority of the church and Christians
seemed to wane, we sought and found ways to compromise
and appease the culture. The general public, especially
in the South, delights in *talking* about Christian faith and
even buying books about it.[21]

In 2002, *Publisher's Weekly* noted that for the
first time in history, the best-selling non-fiction book and
the best-selling fiction book were both from Christian
publishers.[22] Pressed to accommodate, perhaps in
a vain attempt to retain our importance, Christians
emphasized the wrong things – e.g., politics, particular
candidates, stem cell research, monuments to the
Ten Commandments, etc. We in the church are guilty
of playing our own star game – allowing the cult of
personality to dominate churches, denominations, the
religious music scene, the Christian book market. One
scholar accuses: Concessions intended to make Christ

more palatable to an increasingly secular public may have secularized and commodified Christianity in order to keep numbers in our churches, to keep selling Christian books, to keep at least some level of the society's focus on our faith.[23] "The issue is not that evangelical Christians are tainted by interaction with secular culture, but rather that the boundary between 'secular' and 'evangelical' has become ever more permeable as evangelical media have grown over the past twenty years."[24]

Culture, the silent language, threatens every Baptist college and university and every university leader. When most of our institutions were founded, it was common to link higher education to religious purposes. We could be proud of the fact that even many a state university sprang directly from, or from familiarity with, evangelical colleges.

Many a state university charter originally had something in it about building character, about God-given truth, or some such phrase. In the 1890s almost every state university required chapel and many required Sunday church attendance. Identification with a local church was common and state university presidents were often ministers. (E.g., from its founding in 1820 to 1900, every University of Alabama president was an ordained minister, mostly Baptist, including Basil Manly.)

But as colleges and universities became more sophisticated, as Darwinism rose to importance, as higher criticism of the Scriptures became more commonly known, the culture began to shift and so did the willingness to be identified with Christianity and with the church. According to George Marsden, the result was that "by the 1920s, the evangelical Protestantism of the old-time colleges had been effectively excluded from leading university classrooms."[25]

As Marsden has so well demonstrated in his book,

The Soul of the American University, it was big-hearted, open, thoughtful individuals who dropped much of the religious influence of our colleges out of a desire to be tolerant, to grant freedom. It became their aspiration to allow freedom of choice and not to make faith compulsory – as if it *could* be. Out of their desire to be inclusive of all views, and to be pluralistic, they came to exclude all religious perspectives.

Specific events hastened the transformation, but the culture was wearing down society's tolerance for church colleges or for Christian influence in state colleges. Among specific influences, we could spend a great deal of time on the new rationalism of the latter nineteenth century, the Scopes trial, and the stress over evolution; the rise of the scientific age; the celebration of youth immediately after World War II and the subsequent rebellion and the defiance of youth in the sixties; the national anger over Vietnam; permissiveness flaunted by the Woodstock generation; the institutional requirements imposed by federal aid.

Well-intentioned, powerful influences slanted our culture from a position that was totally accepting and expecting of heavy religious influence, to a posture of almost disdain for religious concepts within the higher educational institution. Indeed, there seemed to develop almost an inverse index: the more intentionally religious was an institution, obviously the less academically strong it was, and the less respect it tended to garner in academic circles.

The reality is that culture is still working against the believing evangelical Christian. Many individuals in our society would defend our right to believe whatever we desire, including all the tenets dearest to the evangelical heart, but the culture leans against our institutions.

Consider a few ways our culture is foe, rather than friend. First, our society does not warm to people who take their religion seriously – any religion. It is simply not cool to be too much concerned about matters of deep conviction that can so readily distinguish one person from another. The movies, TV, the media? They are all a bit uncomfortable making religion an important subject.

When ABC employed Peggy Wehmeyer, she was the only correspondent of a national news network devoted entirely to religion. Supposedly, in a financial tight, ABC terminated Peggy's contract. Now, for all the money spent on newsgathering in this country, not a single major TV network has a religion correspondent. The big daily newspapers, if they have a religion section, confine it to a once-per-week emphasis, and might not have even that, were it not for the prospect of significant church advertising that tends to come along with it.

A perfect illustration has been the flap over Mel Gibson's movie, *The Passion of Christ*. First, we endured the enormously inflated charges that the film was anti-Semitic. The media appeared to enjoy playing "gotcha." Then, there was amazement at the film's box office success, but no one knew quite what to say about it. Generally, the media found certain extremes to report, and then stepped back to a roster of quotations from people who were impressed by it and from people who were merely mystified by it. It seemed newsworthy, but they did not know how to fit such a powerful message about Jesus into their generalist approach.

We have to admit that a civilization that prides itself on pluralism and diversity cannot focus on one particular religion, let alone the strong convictions of evangelical Christianity. Our society likes soft, friendly, cozy words about religion – values, faith, virtues, etc., but it is uncomfortable with confessional religion or profound claims. *Touched By An Angel* is about as hard core religious as the networks can abide.

Thus, if our society refuses to respect and exalt Jesus, why should we be surprised if it does not sanction and condone OUR devotion to Jesus. (As Duane Litfin and David Dockery, our previous lecturers have urged, if Jesus is to be Lord of each of us, and Lord of our institutions, we cannot expect society to be impressed with that confession, nor to respect and esteem us for it.) After three decades in this role as president of a Baptist college, I conclude that there are many people, even many *Christian* people, who are uneasy about organized religion, embarrassed about being too public about Jesus Christ, and not likely to risk being too closely identified with our institutions. The more obviously Christian our institutions are, the less appealing we are to the broad public.[26]

Of Size, Sports, & Money

Another way culture works against Christian higher education is size. While most of our institutions are smaller than the state universities, our society sees significance in numbers. It assumes that no university would *actually choose* to be small. Even in church circles, perhaps because of our devotion to the concept of church-growth (after all, what church would *not* want to grow?), we expect every institution wants to enroll more. Ask a newspaper editor which is more important: a city of 15,000 or a city of 1,500? Which has greater significance: a business with gross sales of $150 million or $50 million? Which would you rather have move to your city: a plant employing 1,500 persons, or a plant employing 150?

You see, ever so subtly, our culture values big numbers – numbers which most of us do not have.

Those prejudices support another cultural force that opposes us: publicity and recognition. We are fortunate that many of our institutions are cited in *U.S. News & World Report*'s rankings. But we know that other rankings have looked askance at universities with required chapel, required religion courses, etc. We all know certain accrediting and recognition agencies that still doubt that our Christian standards do not interfere with quality academics. And most of us have faced foundation executives, eager to have their foundations' names listed among supporters of big-name universities but skeptical about whether our institutions are worthy.

Of course, there is the subject of sports. Each of us lives in a state which has big athletic powers. People who claim to be deeply committed to Christ, in the vise-grip of our culture, find major athletic events such as football games prime spots for doing business, for making the social scene, for making contact with old friends. I cannot explain the grip these sports have on folks, even some who never enrolled at the particular institution. Yet, I confess that there is great media appeal in mass events – large arenas and stadiums filled with cheering fans who pay multi-thousand-dollar sums for the privilege of buying a ticket. In a culture that fixes on big events, and mass occasions, the 10,000 at a Baptist college football game holds no special appeal.

Consider the money involved. For example, in 1993, Nike paid the University of North Carolina at Chapel Hill $11 million for five-year exclusive rights to put its Nike swoosh on the UNC uniforms, shoes, coaches' jackets, etc.[27] That is powerful competition for small Baptist colleges.

Now, I would like to tell you that you should cheer

up because you will find affirmation among the people of our Baptist churches. Unfortunately, that is not the case. Our own Baptist people have a hard time granting us the respect we deserve. In a reversal of just the last several years, the major state university, in most regions, is more attractive to prospective students, even among high-income families, than a private, let alone Christian, college or university. [28]

And the student culture tends to be influenced by the name-game. The more prevalent a name, the stronger the brand, the easier it is to decide, just as with politicians and name recognition. So, when a student tells his friends he is thinking about one of our institutions, he is not likely to get reinforcement from peers or family or even guidance counselors.

Truth be told, I dare say most of our close church-going friends believe that each one of us would drop the reins of the college we now hold and run a forty-yard dash to get to be president or provost or chief business or student affairs officer at our local state university. More than a decade ago, I was contacted by a headhunter who wanted my name in the pool of candidates for the presidency of a distinguished institution, well endowed, with no crises. Hardly thinking about it, I said, "I'm afraid I'm not your man. I would not know how to give a cocktail party, and my conscience wouldn't allow it, if I knew how." He seemed surprised, but we talked about that and he assured me that was not a requirement. I told him that for a person with my values and beliefs I was probably where I ought to be. He was mystified, disbelieving – as though thinking, "He doesn't realize what he's rejecting" – but respectful. (I will also say that he never called me again!) Most of us are where we are out of deep personal conviction that is incomprehensible to many.

Stand Firm in Our Christian Distinctives

What shall we do? First, we need to work harder to make our own constituents aware of what our institutions are, and be proud of what we offer. We still have too many devout Baptists in our own areas who have never been on our campuses, met our students and professors, or considered our distinctives. All the public relations efforts we aim at the general public might first be aimed at Baptists.

Secondly, we ought to review our mission statements with a hard eye on the distinctive difference our institutions profess. And if we profess it, does it happen in practice? We need particularity – product differentiation – to show how we are unlike the marketplace. Many such statements are so cliché-ridden they almost smell like mothballs. We highlight a few pious phrases to pacify the sponsoring denomination, phrases such as "Christian context," "Christian environment," or "Christian atmosphere."

Next, we generally appease the faculty, paying homage to the scholarly and academic side, saying something about "academic excellence," despite difficulty citing anything about our institutions that truly excels. Our institutions should not be suffering identity crises. We should know who we are, and whose we are, and be secure in that identity. We cannot expect great institutions to spring from mediocre or fanciful intentions. Mission statements need to be articulated to trustees, to prospective faculty, to all personnel, and to students.

Peter Drucker said, "The first task of the leader is to make sure that everybody sees the mission, hears it, lives it. If you lose sight of your mission, you begin to stumble and it shows very, very fast."[29] Surely, one way to resist the fiery darts of our culture is to know and to have agreed upon what you wish to achieve.

I once visited a college as a consultant. It was in trouble with its primary accreditor and running a significant deficit. It was being accused by federal authorities of some serious financial lapses. It had poorly qualified personnel even on the graduate level. Yet all the blather of the mission statement was about "Christian" and "excellence," "finest" and "best." When confronted, the president told me, "Well, that's what we're aiming for." Associating our institutions with the God of the universe, we need to be certain that we are working to be exceptional institutions. Truthfulness is required. Shabbiness –in academics, in the physical campus, in treatment of individuals, in administrative practices – is not worthy of our Lord. Where we are uncomfortable about weaknesses, we should move to correct them. Where claims are overstated, we should change them. And we should have the courage NOT to participate in practices that compromise our integrity! And if we had time, we could have a rousing discussion on the ethics of tuition discounting, as currently practiced.

The Christian College: The Last Best Hope

Well, you might ask, are there any words of encouragement? A number of years ago, I was in a small group of Christian college presidents that met with Dr. Martin Marty. In our society, Marty asked, where could we find anyone to encourage faith development in the young? Of course, the church. But, he pointed out, the church has young people for such a short time – only a few hours a week at best, and then only for a couple of years. What about the media, he asked. Could newspapers, magazines, and TV promote faith development? After a litany of such possibilities, he concluded that the Christian college may be the last best hope for promoting the development of a vibrant personal faith that is strong enough to last. That is a noble purpose. Let us hold to it and not shrink from claiming it.

Two other points for your own personal mental health. Seize that high ground and remind yourself that there is solid, reasonable justification for our Baptist colleges and universities. "Civilization is doomed unless the hearts and minds of men can be changed, and unless we can bring about a moral, intellectual and spiritual reformation."[30] That was not spoken by Billy Graham, but by Robert Maynard Hutchins . . . in 1947.

Who has the greatest chance at that sort of reformation, if not Baptist colleges? Back in the 1950s, there was no correlation between a college education and religious belief, according to surveys. By the 1970s, the college-educated were far less likely than others in this country to attend religious services or hold Christian views.[31] Shall we give over the educated – surrender them to the culture?

Make your peace with the reality that your institution is not like all others; it has a higher and holier calling – no matter the bias of the culture. And make your peace with the reality that the recognition and respect bestowed on other institutions may never be yours in a culture like ours. But then, you are not accountable for being popular with the local Chamber of Commerce. "When the trumpet of the Lord shall sound, and Time shall be no more," you will account to the Lord God for your stewardship. Therefore, be certain that, if Baptist colleges were someday, somehow, to be outlawed, we would see one another in jail.

References:

1 John 17:16-18; I Cor. 5:10; Colossians 2:8, 20.

2 Candy Gunther Brown, *The Word In the World* (Chapel Hill: The University of North Carolina Press, 2004), 6.

3 "In Christ, therefore, they [Christians] claimed to possess a principle of understanding superior to anything existing in the classical world. By this claim they were prepared to stand or fall." Charles Norris Cochrane, *Christianity and Culture* (London: Oxford University Press, 1957), vi. "This is not a struggle to be settled by mere blows, as though the contending forces were nothing more than masses in motion. Nor is it a mere battle of abstract ideas, to be conducted in the rarefied atmosphere of the academies. What it demands is a united effort of hand and heart and head, in order to expose the fictitious character of secular valuations and to vindicate the reality of Christian claims." Ibid., 516.

4 Definitions of culture are many and varied. Taking some concepts from Edward T. Hall, *The Silent Language* (New York: Doubleday, 1959), 169-170, we can consider key elements: "Culture is communication and communication is culture." "Culture is not one thing, but many." "Culture is concerned more with messages than it is with networks and control systems." "There is no experience independent of culture against which culture can be measured." "Cultural indeterminacy and cultural relativity are not easy concepts . . . They mean more than what is good by one set of standards may be bad by some other."

5 Nathan Hatch, historian of American Christianity, states that ". . . plausible arguments can be made that, at all levels of American society, the juggernaut of secularism rolls on, pressing religious belief into smaller, less consequential territory." Nathan Hatch, *The Democratization of American Christianity* (New Haven: Yale University Press, 1989), 211.

6 Quoted in George M. Marsden, *The Soul of the American University* (New York: Oxford University Press, 1994), 401.

7 "The 100 Most Influential People," *TIME* (April 26, 2004).

8 Of course, Christian colleges and universities could be mentioned as having benefited from church support. I believe it likely that, while

the influence of the Christian college has been qualitative, rather than quantitative, we could find that strong leadership in the church, overwhelmed as it may be by the culture, has still come from the ranks of Christian colleges and universities.

[9] Jonathan A. Knee, *The New York Times* (May 2, 2004).

[10] The churchmanship of Kenneth Lay, former CEO of Enron, son of a Baptist minister, and trustee of Houston's First United Methodist Church has been extensively profiled. Richard Scrushy, former Chairman and CEO of HealthSouth, and his wife have been photographed carrying a Bible into the courtroom and have been regular attendees at Mountaintop Church in Birmingham, Alabama. Greg Garrison story released by Religious News Service, (May 30, 2003).

[11] www.Barna.org

[12] Edward T. Hall, *The Silent Language* (1959).

[13] Hall said, " . . . the ultimate purpose of this book . . . is to reveal the broad extent to which culture controls our lives." 38.

[14] John Steele Gordon, "The Fifty Biggest Changes in the Last 50 Years," *American Heritage* (June-July, 2004), 23.

[15] Gordon, "The Fifty Biggest Changes," 24.

[16] One site, SubservientChicken.com, is an interactive view of a person in a chicken suit, who responds to the viewer's computer commands, a subtle ad for Burger King. The ad agency that created the site says it has received more than 215 million hits, with the average visitor remaining at the site for seven minutes. Rob Walker, "Poultry-Geist: If we're so sick of marketing, why are we watching this chicken?" *New York Times Magazine* (May 23, 2004), 18.

[17] The ability to customize such communications is amazing and sometimes alarming. *Reason Magazine*, to emphasize its story on "databasification," in its June 2004, issue, individually personalized 40,000 subscriber copies with a cover featuring the subscriber's name in large type, an aerial photo of the subscriber's neighborhood, with the subscriber's actual residence/office circled. Inside, certain facts such as average daily commuting time for that ZIP code, average income, etc., were cited.

[18] "Changing Minds Winning Peace," The Advisory Group on Public Diplomacy in the Arab and Muslim World (Washington, D.C., 2003), 21.

[19] The cases of Andrea Yates, Kobe Bryant, Mary Kay LeTourneau, and Vili Fualaau (1992), and Elizabeth Smart received extensive and repetitive coverage in daily newspapers, news magazines, etc.

[20] I am not quite as pessimistic as some. "Some critics argue that the seductive culture spawned by television and related communications technologies has already obliterated, beyond repair, the very premises of democratic promise." William Greider, *Who Will Tell the People: The Betrayal of American Democracy* (New York: Simon & Schuster, 1992), 312. "If the mass-media culture has permanently robbed people of their democratic capacities, then the deeper governing problems – or their remedies – will have no meaning to ordinary citizens." Ibid., 313.

[21] " . . . [T]he United States contains more citizens who value religion than other western industrial societies." Nathan Hatch, *The Democratization of American Christianity,* 210.

[22] Bruce Wilkinson's *The Prayer of Jabez* and Tim F. LaHaye's and Jerry B. Jenkins's *Desecration: Antichrist Takes the Throne,* eighth in the *Left Behind* series. Cited in Brown, 243.

[23] "By degrees religion itself took on the shape of a commodity . . . [It] looked for ways to appeal to all consumers using the techniques of advertising and publicity employed by other merchants." R. Laurence Moore, *Selling God: American Religion In the Marketplace of Culture* (New York: Oxford University Press, 1994), 6.

[24] Heather Hendershot, *Shaking the World for Jesus* (Chicago: University of Chicago Press, 2004), 24.

[25] George Marsden, *The Soul of the American University,* 4.

[26] Hatch, himself a prominent academic, as provost of The University of Notre Dame, wrote, "In the world of higher education, theologians and church leaders no longer operate from a position of strength. To avoid being considered second-class citizens, they are pressured to make accommodations to the secular definition of values at the core of the university." Nathan Hatch, *The Democratization of American Christianity,* 119.

[27] Murray Sperber, "College Sports, Inc.: How Big-Time Athletic Departments Run Interference for College, Inc.," in Donald G. Stein, *Buying In or Selling Out* (Piscataway, NJ: Rutgers University Press, 2004), 24.

[28] "Suddenly, State Universities Have More Allure," *The New York*

Times (November 10, 2002).

[29] Peter Drucker, *Managing the Nonprofit Organization* (New York: HarperCollins, 1990), 45.

[30] Quoted in George Marsden, *The Soul of the American University*, 408.

[31] Robert Wuthnow, *The Struggle for America's Soul: Evangelicals, Liberals, and Secularism* (Grand Rapids: Wm. B. Eerdmans, 1989), 34-35.

Editor's Note:

*Chapter 1 is an edited version of Tom Corts's H.I. Hester
Lecture delivered in 2004, two years before his retirement
from the Samford University presidency. On June 6, 2010,
I was given the privilege of delivering the H.I. Hester
Lecture at the meeting of the International Association
of Baptist Colleges and Universities. An edited version of
those remarks constitutes this chapter.*

CHAPTER 2

TRANSFORMING LIVES

By Paul R. Corts

What a wonderful honor it is to be here with you today. I am humbled by your invitation to deliver one of the H. I. Hester lectures. Dr. Hester was a very important leader in Baptist higher education at a crucial point in our history, encouraging our Baptist higher education community to embrace a strong commitment to rigorous intellectual inquiry in contrast to the sentiments of many of his era who favored anti-intellectualism. The litany of godly thought-leaders and teachers who have delivered Hester lectures at this meeting and at several Baptist institutions is a who's who listing to which I might aspire, but will never be worthy to be listed.

I have known the vast majority of you for much of your professional careers in Christian higher education, and it is intimidating to be asked to deliver a thoughtful address to people who know you so well; for you know me, warts and all. I began attending these meetings in the 1970s, and many great presidents – some who have now passed on – befriended me and made an incredible investment in my life. Ben Fisher and Arthur Walker were two senior educators who shared a lot of mature wisdom with this young upstart, and I had the good fortune to be a colleague of Bob Agee, a dear friend and wonderful encourager. When my brother Tom was asked to lead this organization, he called to talk with me about it, and we quizzically wondered together – could it really be? Of course since he had so generously been my big brother mentor throughout my career, I proudly knew he fit the role.

The Mission of Transforming Lives

But alas, I reminisce. We must move on to this important topic I have been assigned – the mission of Christ-centered higher education to transform lives. An important lesson we learn from these giants of Christian higher education is the incredibly important role of our institutional presidents in stewarding their institutions during their period of leadership, maintaining the Christian focus in the mission of the school, and leading in such a way as to preserve a pervasive Christian influence throughout the entirety of the campus culture. Indeed, we have been blessed by those heroes of the faith who were obedient to God's calling. From the early founding years they became stewards of the sacred trust in leading our Baptist colleges and universities that we have inherited today. They prayed earnestly, sacrificed in ways that we can barely imagine in the affluence of our times; and although the lights dimmed on several occasions, with their scrappy determination and God's favor they simply would not allow the lights of Christian higher education to go out. Yet today, as most of higher education in America has lost its way and deserted its heritage of faith, losing sight of its reason for being, we are especially thankful to be the beneficiaries of those faithful stewards who followed the admonition of Scripture to preserve and grow "the faith that was once for all entrusted to the saints" (Jude 3).

Early American higher education sought to develop students to have the mind of Christ, following Scripture's admonition. The Apostle Paul urged the church at Rome, "Do not conform any longer to the pattern of this world, but be transformed by the renewing of your mind" (Rom. 12:2). In Philippians, we are challenged, "Let this mind be in you, which was also in Christ Jesus" (Philippians 2:5). Collegiate learning was designed to help students learn to love God with all their minds. When Jesus was asked to name the greatest commandment of all, He responded. "The most important one," answered Jesus, "is this: 'Hear, O Israel, the Lord our God, the Lord is one. Love the Lord your God with all your heart and with all your soul and with all your mind and with all your strength. The second is this: 'Love your neighbor as yourself.' There is no commandment greater than these" (Mark 12:29-31).

Higher education in America has a very rich tradition of commitment to the moral and spiritual development of its students to help them think and live Christianly. Many of the emerging leaders of the new world in America wanted a more just society built on Christian principles and were motivated to create educational institutions that would ensure a well-educated core of leaders educated in a biblical worldview context. This biblical grounding gave them a firm understanding of truth, of right and wrong, and how one should live. But this historic foundational understanding that propelled all of American higher education for its first 250 years, is what the higher education elite has since jettisoned.

Albert Meyer, for many years head of the Mennonite board for higher education and himself a scientist, in his book *Realizing our Intentions*, helps us understand the challenge we face in the landscape of contemporary higher education. "At the heart of any higher education is, after all, a conception of truth."[1]

We affirm that Scripture teaches that Jesus told His disciples, "If you hold to my teaching, you are really my disciples. Then you will know the truth, and the truth will set you free" (John 8:31b-32). Truth is not an abstract concept; rather Christ is the very embodiment of Truth. Jesus said, "I am the way, the truth, and the life" (John 14:6a). Christ-centered higher education has at its core Christ – who is Truth. And that puts us right where the beginning of higher education in America started. Harvard's early *Rules and Precepts that are observed in the Colledge* states that the primary aim of a Harvard education was for students to "know God and Jesus Christ, which is eternal life, John 17:3, and therefore to lay Christ in the bottom, as the foundation of all sound knowledge and learning."[2]

Meyer notes, "The Enlightenment thought around us has assumed, at least until the deconstructionism of the recent past, that reality consists of autonomous objects 'out there.' To arrive at the truth according to this understanding we need to handle the objects 'out there' from a distance in order to minimize our subjective biases. We need to develop propositions that conform to the canons of evidence and reason about such objects, and we need to break down objects into pieces and sub-pieces for analysis in order to get to what they really are."

He points to Parker Palmer's observation that "when Jesus was brought before Pilate to be tried, Pilate said to Jesus, 'So you are a king?' Jesus answered, 'You say that I am a king. For this I was born, and for this I have come into the world, to bear witness to the truth. Everyone who is of the truth hears My voice.' Pilate said to Him, 'What is truth?'"[3]

> Commenting on this question, Palmer exhorts:
> Pilate's final question can be asked with a cynical sneer or a despairing sigh, or both. But the cynicism and despair are not to be located in the word 'truth' . . . The problem is in the word 'what.' . . . From the outset. . . Pilate tried to reduce Jesus to an object by forcing him in the category of 'king,' thus making him both comprehensible and dispensable in the political framework of the time . . . . Pilate is the model objectivist, focusing on the 'whatness' of truth, while before him stands a person in whom truth is embodied, a person who is not an object 'out there,' but a subject who wants to enter into Pilate's life . . . . By reducing truth to nonpersonal terms, Pilate puts truth beyond reach, and finally assents to that violence which wants to murder truth.[4]

In many ways we are in unfriendly territory because we have at our core a very different understanding of the most fundamental concept of all – truth. Palmer says, "When academics speak of 'the pursuit of truth,' . . . there is a conceit hidden in that image: that we can close the gap by tracking an elusive truth down. This gap exists not because truth is evasive but because we are . . . Subjective truth is truth to which we subject ourselves . . . . The objectivist approach to education is so tenacious because it is a defense against transformation."[5]

But from a polar opposite we approach our mission of Christ-centered higher education with transformation as our core intention. We pursue our mission through a commitment to holistic education, nurturing the intellect, shaping and molding the heart and soul, modeling servanthood as a way of life, and touching our neighbors throughout the world with a touch of the love of God. We believe that a college or university education can and usually will have a significant formative impact on the development of a student's whole person, and we want that persona to bear the likeness of Christ.

Some would say that we are regular colleges and universities, doing what every other college or university does, with perhaps a little extra in the area of moral or character development with a sectarian dose of religion – and it is that little dose of religion that is so objectionable to the secularist who believes religion as a spiritual phenomena or belief system affecting one's understanding of truth has no place in the halls of true learning. But we call that whole person education spiritual formation, shaping the moral character of students. We do not believe in the secularists' contention that things spiritual must be isolated into a silo to be kept separate from the intellectual and outside of academe. Our spiritual formation concerns itself with the development of the whole person – the intellectual, spiritual, emotional, physical, and social – as we seek to help students learn how to think and live following the model of Christ.

Now we should take particular note that Paul in his letter to the Romans, when he urges the renewal of the mind, immediately goes on with the explanation of the body of Christ, the church, with many members and each with unique and special gifts. Those special gifts run the gambit of being intellectual, spiritual, emotional, physical, and social, but with intricate interrelationships that allow the whole body of the church to be more than the sum of its parts and thus to have a powerful impact for good on the world and ultimately to overcome evil with good. Likewise, spiritual formation in the image of Christ seeks to develop the whole person while celebrating the particular gifts and strengths of each individual student, whether traditional-age college student or adult learner.

A Short History of Higher Education

When I joined the Council staff in 2006, I went on a yearlong listening tour of member and affiliate campuses to hear from our constituencies. I learned a lot about the challenges our campuses are facing and many of the concerns held by differing groups. While a very long list of topics and issues grew out of the listening experience, a smaller number stood out as more prevalent and more broadly held.[6] At nearly every institution I heard campus leaders talk about their commitment to a Christian community where Christ is preeminent, where a robust intellectual climate provides students with a superior educational experience, and where faculty and staff are united in seeking to transform the lives of students shaping strong moral character development, and molding them in the image and likeness of the Lord Jesus Christ to think Christianly. It was a gratifying experience that affirmed the existing mission statement of the Council, "to help institutions transform lives by faithfully relating scholarship and service to biblical truth."

If this "transforming lives" is a unifying theme for our institutions, as I believe it is, it represents a stellar identifier for the unique and unusual mission of our institutions only in the sense that we admittedly seek to do that through "relating scholarship and service to biblical truth" with an holistic and integrative approach. I did a quick, informal and unscientific survey of many state supported and non-faith-based private institutions and was surprised to find many using some version of transformation language in their mission or purpose statements, generally however without any reference to moral character development.

While many higher education experts often reference the great mosaic of American higher education as one of our nation's great strengths, Albert Meyer, in his new book *Realizing Our Intentions*, claims that, "In recent decades, private institutions have become more like public ones, and public ones have increasingly become more like private ones." Anthony Kronman, Sterling Professor of Law at Yale and author of *Education's End: Why Our Colleges and Universities Have Given Up on the Meaning of Life*, on the other hand, argues that the differences among the more than 6,000 institutions of higher education in America "– of function, character and aim – are so large that 'college' and 'university' are only words they share in common."[7]

Meyer and Kronman, both in their own way, have valid perspectives, and while expressing their views in very different ways, both do seem to agree that most of those 6,000 institutions have given up on teaching the meaning of life. Do we really believe that during critical formative years, university age students will not be struggling with big questions like the meaning of life? Surely they will, but most will be attending universities that will not be intentionally helping them develop their own personal understanding of the great questions of life. However, students attending Christian colleges and universities will find that the core mission of their institutions is to help students with spiritual formation through intentionally encouraging, supporting, and helping them develop their views on the big questions of the meaning of life.

Back to our history, higher education was born in America by Christians with a very profound Christian mission, and the vast majority of all the institutions created in the early centuries of our land followed a similar pattern. Indeed, Kronman divides all of American higher education into three periods, with the first period from the founding of Harvard until after the Civil War. He concludes that "the ends of human living are not merely a fit subject of instruction, but the one subject above all others ... [and] instruction on the meaning of life proceeded on the basis of dogmatic assumptions that were simply taken for granted."[8]

Kronman does not say, but we should add that the aim of education then was just what he calls for now – to teach people the meaning of life. Those early founders did that by pointing them to the only Person on earth who lived a perfect life, the Lord Jesus Christ. Kronman refers to their use of "dogmatic assumptions" to help guide students, and those assumptions are biblical truth claims articulated by Jesus and Holy Scripture. The founders sought to provide an educational community that would encourage students to develop their moral character by following the One who taught radical paradoxes, such as it is in giving that we receive, and to find life we must be willing to give away our lives in service to others.

A key aim of virtually all higher education was moral and spiritual formation of students to live lives of high character that would model Christ and support the public good. Great diversity in higher education in America came much later, especially with the rise of governmentally supported higher education in the late nineteenth century and then the rise of humanistic secularism among the private elite institutions.

As I previously indicated, higher education in America started with the Puritans' founding of Harvard College in 1636 with a pledge to teach every student that the primary purpose of life and study "is to know God and Jesus Christ which is eternal life, John 17:3, and therefore to lay Christ in the bottom, as the foundation of all sound knowledge and learning."[9] This noble beginning of higher education in North America was distinctly, profoundly, completely Christ-centered. It was to be transformational, designed to shape students in the image of Christ so that their thinking and living would be like Christ's. The Harvard rules of that era make it plain that this was to be an extremely rigorous education to know the Truth and possess understanding in the context of eternal consequences.

In the early eighteenth century, Congregational clergy founded Yale; Presbyterians founded Princeton; Baptists – Brown; the Dutch Reformed – Rutgers; and Congregationalists – Dartmouth. In addition to rigorous studies in the Bible, these institutions also offered the liberal arts through the eyes of faith from a biblical and Christian perspective, with a mission to educate the whole person in mind and spirit, equipping them to live lives of moral integrity and service to others and society.

The nineteenth century brought the Second Great Awakening and spiritual renewal to colleges like Yale and Princeton but also a tidal wave of enthusiasm for planting new Christian colleges. Baptists were among the most active in birthing new institutions. The twentieth century saw the rapid emergence of the Bible college movement, many of them identifying with fundamentalism and the battle against modernism. Most Protestant colleges were squeaking by during the Great Depression and World War II, but a number did not survive. Following the war, higher education, including Christian colleges and universities, boomed as the GI Bill flooded schools with bright, energetic veterans. The post-war influx of students grew financial resources in the 1950s and '60s, allowing the new breed of Christian colleges to excel and gain credibility. In 1971, the ten-member Christian College Consortium met for the first time, declaring its intent "to promote the purposes of evangelical Christian higher education . . ."[10]

By this time, as we have discussed, modernism had worked its charm of deception, demanding that the mind and the heart be separated, and most of the great historic institutions founded on Christ and the Bible had become secularized. By the end of the twentieth century, writers like George Marsden in his work, *The Soul of the American University*, provided a brilliant though sobering commentary on the role of Christian faith and Protestant churches in the establishment and development of America's early and leading private and public universities, only to see the eventual eviction of faith from the halls of these great universities. James Burtchaell's *The Dying of the Light* chronicles exhaustively in nearly a thousand pages a much larger swath of Protestant and Catholic colleges and universities that were lovingly created and supported by their Christian churches until that relationship was "severed," to use Burtchaell's term, mostly during the mid to late twentieth century.

I suppose we could say some institutions sold their institutional souls for a mess of pottage, trading faith for an allegiance to secularism. While there are many writings expounding on how and why this happened, it is still puzzling to me. I appreciate Stephen Carter's sentiment on this. He says, ". . . it is not easy, in a nation committed to religious liberty, to understand why the risk that the religions might try to impose on secular society their religious visions of the good life is more to be avoided than the risk that the state and its powerful constituents might try to impose on the religions a secular vision of the good life."[11]

The Big Issues like the Meaning of Life

I have mentioned already Anthony Kronman and his *Education's End: Why our Colleges and Universities Have Given Up on the Meaning of Life.* Discussing his book with the publication *Inside Higher Ed,* Kronman gave a crisp response to the question posed in the title of his book, saying that professors at most of America's public and private universities find "the question of life's meaning . . . too large, too sprawling, too personal to be a subject that any specialized scholar feels comfortable tackling."[12] Kronman provides an interesting historical description of American higher education's desertion from dealing with the meaning of life by identifying three distinct periods in American higher education, chronicling the drift away from teaching about the meaning of life. He laments the "directionlessness that prevails at most colleges and universities" and remarks that "the appetite for such a venture [teaching about the meaning of life] may very well be greater at our country's less elite schools."[13] I applaud Kronmen for his passion in making the case for this perspective we share – that higher education should be helping students deal with questions about the meaning of life – even though we would approach how to do that in quite different ways.

Following publication of Kronman's book, Yale's president Richard Levin told Yale freshmen assembled with their parents at the opening of the school year in 2007, "The four years ahead of you offer a once-in-a-lifetime opportunity to pursue your intellectual interests wherever they may lead, and, wherever they may lead, you will find something to reflect upon that is pertinent to your quest for meaning in life. It is true that your professors are unlikely to give you the answers to questions about what you should value and how you should live. We leave the answers up to you."[14] We agree with Levin on that point, as what one values and how one chooses to live are questions that ultimately must be answered by every individual personally, but as Christian colleges and universities we do not capitulate nor shrink from the responsibility to teach about "the good life," personal responsibility, civic duty, justice, love, compassion and care for others, and a host of other Christian values so clearly articulated by Christ in his teachings and demonstrated by Christ in his living.

I found it fascinating that Levin, after advising, "We leave the answers up to you," tells the audience of his personal commitment as a faculty member to seek to transform lives by encouraging a worldview through the eyes of economics. He goes on to say:

> Long ago, I taught introductory economics in Yale College. I always began by telling the students that the course would change their lives. I still believe this. Why? Because economics will open you to an entirely new and different way of understanding how the world works. Economics won't prescribe for you how society should be organized, or the

extent to which individual freedom should be subordinated to collective ends, or how the fruits of human labor should be distributed – at home and around the world. But understanding the logic of markets will give you a new way to think about these questions, and, because life is lived within society and not in abstraction from it, economics will help you to think about what constitutes a good life.[15]

Levin acknowledges that in his course he was trying to shape the students' lives since he resolutely claims that the course would "change their lives" and "understanding the logic of markets will give you a new way to think." We believe an encounter with the living Christ will *change their lives* and understanding biblical Christian faith will give students *a new way to think* – to think Christianly. So President Levin is solidly in our camp that it *is* possible for university education to shape and form how one understands and thinks and thus how one responds personally to the question of the meaning of life.

While President Levin allows that economics, his field of expertise, can help you answer the big question about the meaning of life, he makes no mention in his address that faith could play a role nor any acknowledgement of a role for moral, ethical, and spiritual truths. Our Christian colleges and universities provide education in all the disciplines similar to all the rest of higher education, but we approach learning and education in a holistic and integrative way with moral, ethical, and spiritual dimensions from a Christian worldview perspective. We believe an understanding of the teachings of Jesus and a commitment to follow Jesus as a disciple can help students discover in a very personal way the meaning of life for them as a unique person created in the image of Almighty God, as well as prepare them to live a moral and virtuous life as a citizen of the world.

In an opinion piece written for the *Boston Globe*, Kronman speaks of his lament that this meaning of life question has been ignored by most of higher education, and claims, "This abandonment has also helped create a society in which deeper questions of values are left in the hands of those motivated by religious conviction – a disturbing and dangerous development." One wonders if those deeper questions of values are less dangerous when left in the hands of passionate economists like Levin? Kronman acknowledges, "The question of life's meaning is a worry of the spirit." He goes on to say, "Our culture may be spiritually impoverished, but what it needs is not more religion. What it needs is an alternative to religion, for colleges and universities to become again the places they once were – spiritually serious but non-dogmatic, concerned with the soul but agnostic about God."[16] Kronman's sweeping statements about religion reflect a view that appears hostile, but he notes that Socrates and Jesus "were able to keep this question before themselves with a steadiness the rest of us can never attain. We are drawn to them for this reason, quite apart from the substance of their teachings. We are fascinated by their ability to pursue the question of life's meaning with such unflagging seriousness . . . ."[17] Naturally, I applaud Kronman's praise for Jesus, while I am puzzled by his passionate belief that the non-spiritual world of academe can be a substitute to the spiritual world of religion to provide for the rebirth of spiritual development of students, an apparent view of utter separation of mind and spirit (at least religious spirit), and his indication that religion has no place in university education.

My brother Tom, in a Hester Lecture he delivered in 2004 and after articulating the way our culture has turned against much of organized religion and Christian principles, shared this view:

Thus, if our society refuses to respect and exalt Jesus, why should we be surprised if it does not sanction and condone OUR devotion to Jesus. (As Duane Litfin and David Dockery, our previous lecturers have urged, if Jesus is to be Lord of each of us, and Lord of our institutions, we cannot expect society to be impressed by that confession, nor to respect and esteem us for it!) After three decades in this role as president of a Baptist college, I conclude that there are many people, even many *Christian* people, who are uneasy about organized religion, embarrassed about being too public about Jesus Christ, and not likely to risk being too closely identified with our institutions. The more obviously Christian our institutions are, the less appealing we are to the broad public."[18]

While much of society and many of our great historic institutions have been sucked into a false belief in the separation of mind and spirit, Christ-centered schools have followed the Lord's great commandment: To love the Lord our God with all of our heart and soul and mind and strength. Great Christian universities like those represented here today have stood firm, unashamedly demonstrating that a strong commitment to high academic standards and the search for truth should, can, and must go hand-in-hand with taking on the mind of

Christ, who is The Truth. In answer to the question "How should you live?" these Christian colleges and universities have a plain, straightforward answer: It is "Follow Christ!" That's the all-important goal of Christ-centered higher education.

What Does the Future Hold?

So, it is fair to ask, what should we be doing in these days of our leadership of Christian higher education? If I were giving two Hester Lectures, I would take up this topic in detail in the next lecture. But since I am confined to one lecture, let me briefly mention a direction I think we should take.

First, we should focus on the mission with laser-like intensity and a fierce commitment. In a report titled *Keeping the Main Thing*, I urge our schools to hold fast to their Christ-centered mission. Our society needs Christian colleges more desperately than it realizes. And we are full of hope for the future. For the past twenty years Christian universities have grown at a far faster pace than any other segment of higher education. Interest in spiritual phenomena has risen sharply.

Second, we need to be sure we know what we mean when we say our institutions want to transform lives. The Council has embarked on an ambitious research agenda to define spiritual formation as understood and practiced among our institutions so that we can have some unity around a very basic core definition that also allows each institution to expand the definition to suit their unique.

Third, we need to identify what it is that we are doing at our schools that contributes to the fulfillment of the transforming lives mission. What programs, activities, actions, and learning experiences do we design, implement, and foster to help realize spiritual formation? Are they actually accomplishing the aspects of spiritual formation that we say they are designed to do?

Fourth, we must answer the question, "Are we graduating students whose lives have been transformed?" We need to work together to gather common data to demonstrate to a skeptical, secular public that wants to hold our institutions accountable that we are accomplishing the religious mission that we claim. While there is much good research that has been done in measuring spiritual development, we need a common data set and a sustained group commitment. Our institutions have a treasure of anecdotal human-interest stories that are great testimonies, but they will not win the day in the court of public accountability. Again, this is a key ingredient in the Council's research agenda on spiritual formation.

Fifth, we have to do a better job of developing the governance component of our institutions. When we were doing a self-study of our Council's work, we realized that we were devoting almost no resources to perhaps one of the most important aspects of our institutions, especially when it comes to keeping the mission on track – support for our governing boards. Our studies of governance boards show much that is very worrisome, and those who have chronicled institutional drift have well documented the role of governing boards and their members in that tragedy. The Council has just launched a new Trustee Development Curriculum to help our institutions better educate and develop their governing board members on key issues of governance, especially important for Christ-centered colleges and universities.

Sixth, we must do a better job of communicating the value and worth of what we do. The Council conducts a major market research project every few years and the latest one has revealed some frightening statistics about changes in how Christian colleges are perceived. Church-going families are concerned about the cost of Christian higher education and fret that Christian colleges may not be worth the price. Among these families who are at the exploratory stage of choosing a college, the desire to have their student nurtured in a Christian university environment has slipped, while on the other hand the objective to have their student go to a university that will help them get a good, high-paying job has risen to the top of the list. It is not or does not have to be an either or. We need the research to confirm what we anecdotally believe and that will demonstrate our institutions provide their students with a great quality education and good job opportunities, as well as an education about how to think and live Christianly.

Going Forward with Confidence

I conclude my remarks assuring you of my great optimism for the future of our movement. Students at our great Christian universities like yours are incredibly blessed. On our campuses and through our extended programs they are surrounded by a Christian community and culture, traditional or cyber, by faculty and administration who consider it a vocational calling to serve them, by alumni and friends who love and support that community, by churches and people of faith that help provide for you. To whom much is given, much is expected. Hebrews reminds us that we are surrounded by a great cloud of witnesses – followers of Christ who stepped out in faith and obedience to found our institutions, and the thousands who have nurtured and sustained Christian institutions through the years. Today we are entrusted to steward and sustain these sacred places, but more quickly than we can possibly grasp, we will pass on the mantle of leadership to the very generation that has been under our tutelage.

Everywhere I go, as I travel the globe visiting our institutions, I hear the marvelous stories of the transformed lives of Christian college alumni who are having a huge impact for good, both here at home and around the world, serving as Christ taught. Each of your institutions has a hall of fame of alumni who have made extraordinary breakthroughs in a wide number of professions and areas who are only representative of the thousands and thousands of your other alumni who live resolutely Christian lives of service that are touching the world for good with the love of God.

Transforming lives – our institutions are still committed to the historic mission of Christ-centered higher education. We are still in the business of encouraging students to know the Lord Jesus Christ personally, to seek Him with all their hearts, and to think and live Christianly. Wherever He leads – follow Christ!

The great hymn writer painted a word picture for us: Were all the oceans filled with ink, were all the people on earth professional writers, were all the skies of the heavens paper, to write the love of God would drain the oceans, overflow all the pages of paper, and wear out all the professional writers, but it would only have just begun to tell the story of God's love. It is impossible to put into words the enormity of the impact that Christian higher education has had in sharing God's love through the centuries and all over the world, but we praise God for its faithful ministry. May each of us, today's generation of leaders, accept the mantle of stewardship for this sacred trust of Christ-centered higher education, and may we be found faithful to run the race with perseverance – keeping our eyes fixed on Jesus, staying Christ-centered, and mindful that we are cheered on by that great cloud of witnesses who faithfully went before us.

References:

1   Albert J. Meyer, *Realizing Our Intentions* (Abilene: Abilene Christian University Press, 2009), 92.

2   Benjamin Pierce, *A History of Harvard University, from its foundation, in the year 1636, to the period of the American Revolution* (Cambridge: Brown, Shattuck & Co., 1833), "Rules and Precepts that are observed in the Colledge." Appendix 5.

3   Albert Meyer, *Realizing*, 92.

4   Albert Meyer, *Realizing*, 93.

5   Albert Meyer, *Realizing*, 93. These Parker citations by Meyer are from Parker J. Palmer, "Truth is Personal: A Deeply Christian Education," *The Christian Century*, 21 Oct. 1981: 1051-55.

6   The Listening Tour provided valuable input to the Council's strategic plan, *The Blueprint for the Future*. Completed and approved by the Board of Directors in 2008, the document contains six major pillars identifying strategic goals for the Council's work over the next five years.

7   Anthony T. Kronman, *Education's End: Why Our Colleges and Universities Have Given Up on the Meaning of Life* (New Haven: Yale University Press), 37.

8   Anthony Kronman, *Education's End*, 46.

9   Benjamin Pierce, *A History of Harvard*, Appendix 5.

10 James A. Patterson, *Shining Lights: A History of the Council for Christian Colleges & Universities* (Grand Rapids: Baker Academic, 2001).

11 Stephen L. Carter, *The Culture of Disbelief* (New York: Basic Books, 1993), 145.

12 "Elevating the Great Books Anew," *Inside Higher Ed* (September 26, 2007).

13 "Elevating the Great Books Anew."

14 Richard C. Levin, "Freshman Address: The Questions that Matter," Presidential Speeches and Statements 2007, accessed August 14, 2011, http://opac.yale.edu/president/message.aspx?id=2.

15 Richard Levin, "Freshman Address."

16 Anthony Kronman, "Why are we here?" *Boston Globe* (September 16, 2007), accessed August 14, 2011, http://www.boston.com/news/globe/ideas/articles/2007/09/16/why_are_we_here/.

17 Anthony Kronman, *Education's End*, 17.

18 Thomas E. Corts, "The University, the Church, and the Culture," *The Baptist Educator*, Vol. LXIX (First Quarter 2005), 7.

Editor's Note:

Gerald Bray became acquainted with Tom when he came to teach at Samford University's Beeson Divinity School in 1993. Bray tells that he was helping to familiarize Tom with Cambridge, England, while Tom was on sabbatical there when "Tom shared with me his vision of what Samford University ought to become, and it is something of that vision that I am here passing on to a wider public . . . a spiritual vision for the university and the community of students and scholars that it seeks to nurture." Bray, a noted biblical scholar and author, says " . . . it is for this, more than anything else, that he ought to be remembered by all of us who have benefitted so much from that vision."

CHAPTER 3

THE CHALLENGE TO THE MIND IN CHRISTIAN HIGHER EDUCATION TODAY

By Gerald L. Bray

Christians in a Secular World

It is seldom remembered now, but until only two or three generations ago, higher education was so closely intertwined with Christianity that it would have seemed strange to most people to talk about one apart from the other. When Tom Corts entered academic life, he was heir to a long tradition of Christian scholarship and was able to make his own contribution to it in the knowledge that he was working for the church and the church was supporting him.

For centuries, the church had invested in colleges and seminaries, not only to train its own ministers but also to prepare young men (and latterly also women) for many different walks of life. Even in state-funded universities where there was no theological faculty, few would have questioned their fundamentally Christian ethos. Here and there one could have found religious skeptics, but they were eccentric characters whose opinions were not taken very seriously. It is true that growing numbers of biologists and geologists were rejecting the biblical account of creation, but even many of them would have thought of themselves as Christians. The notion that Darwinism pitted science in a life-and-death struggle against faith that would end with the triumph of science is a popular myth that does not really correspond to the facts. Of course, there were literalistic interpreters of Scripture who rejected anything that appeared to contradict the Genesis story, just as there were scientists who reacted to that by becoming atheists. But the majority believed that science and religion were approaching truth from different standpoints, or that there were two different kinds of truth. These did not really conflict with each other because although they were talking about the same things, they were doing so in different ways and with a different purpose in view.

How different it all is now. There are still many scientists and other academics and intellectuals who are Christians, but the Christian worldview that once was taken for granted has all but vanished from the public square. The kind of scholar who would illustrate his points from the Bible, quote from books like Proverbs or conclude with a pious reference to "the Deity" has gone the way of the dodo. Nowadays, any researcher who so much as hints at having a personal faith is accused of being unscholarly. Bringing God into an academic discussion is ruled out as unacceptable in advance. Yet at the same time, militant atheists are given free rein. To mention just one example, at the University of Oxford, whose motto is Dominus illuminatio mea ('The Lord is my light'), one of the best-known professors is Richard Dawkins, whose job is to explain modern science to ordinary people. In practice however, Dawkins spends most of his time attacking religion in all its forms, and particularly Christianity. His arguments are often trite and his behavior in public can be atrocious, but he is allowed to carry on unmolested and even considered by some to be a major thinker of our times.

Nor is Dawkins alone. In recent years a host of lesser characters have jumped on the atheist bandwagon, not least in reaction to the rise of religious fundamentalism, which to them is one of the major evils of our age. The fact that what they have in mind is almost exclusively an Islamic phenomenon, with no real equivalent in the Christian world, is overlooked, and what applies to the former is automatically applied to the latter, because it is religion in general that is the enemy. Bizarre as this seems to believing Christians, it is par for the course in the modern academy, where theology has been replaced by religious studies and faith is a catch-all word that includes anybody or anything that takes religion seriously, regardless of what the particular religion happens to be. Not long ago I was given a thorough search by airport security and had my Bible removed from my hand luggage and closely examined, presumably because possession of such a volume was a sign of potential religious fanaticism. How long will it be before a Bible is confiscated and the person owning it is refused permission to travel? Perhaps things will not go that far, but that it is no longer inconceivable shows how wide the gap now is between the officially-sanctioned culture in which we live and the Christian faith that we continue to profess.

In a world like ours, a Christian university seems to

be an oxymoron and an embarrassment. The intellectual establishment regards it as a contradiction in terms because knowledge is no longer thought to have any connection with faith and is often seen to be in opposition to it. It is embarrassing because many institutions of higher learning have to maintain some kind of link to their religious origins, an obligation that may be written in their charter or linked to their endowment, but the only practical effect of this is that their faculty do all they can to persuade the wider academic community that this religious heritage does not make any real difference. As individuals, they claim the freedom to say and write whatever they want to, even if they have to stand with their heads bowed when the chaplain says a prayer at the opening convocation each semester. The forms of faith are preserved but the substance has departed, and any attempt to bring it back will be met with a barrage of accusations that the academic integrity of the institution is being compromised. In some places it is even taken for granted that incoming students who have a church background will be challenged to think for themselves and so gradually weaned off any serious form of belief. Ironically, a Christian college may thus turn out to be more like an atheist factory managed by people for whom skepticism and unbelief are synonymous with maturity.

But even when this tendency is resisted, the problems facing Christian educators do not go away. Students are still obliged to use textbooks that ignore or undermine their beliefs, and scholars have to engage with a secular academy on its terms, not theirs. Churches may unwittingly make matters worse by insisting on enforcing strict moral guidelines as the chief hallmark of a school's Christian identity, while ignoring or being unable to grasp the need to apply biblical principles to the substance of the academic disciplines being taught there. It is admittedly easier to block access to Internet pornography than it is to work out what to do about global warming, but for that very reason scholars should concentrate more on the latter than on the former. Too often churches are inclined to think of Christian colleges as places where their young people can be protected from the big bad world outside, when they should be more concerned to see that those same young people are shaped by Christian values and principles and taught how to apply them to all aspects of life.

Another problem we face is that there are some influential people today who believe that Christian higher education is no longer necessary. As they see it, it may have served a purpose in the days when university access was severely restricted, but now that most people can go to college, a faith-based institution is liable to be relatively expensive and, therefore, accused of fostering the very elitism that it once tried to overcome. Moreover, even perfectly sincere Christian believers can be heard to argue that Christian students ought to be exposed to the dominant secular world-views of our time so that they can live in the society that those views have created and bear witness to it. There is some merit in this argument, and there is no doubt that a Christian witness is sorely needed on secular campuses, but where will the driving force for that witness come from if there is nowhere that it can develop? The case for having Christian institutions of higher learning is not weakened by the fact that we live in a pluralistic and secular society. On the contrary, it may be stronger than ever and vital if Christian voices are ever going to make themselves heard in the modern world.

The Nature of the University

Universities as we know them today have a Christian origin. There are one or two schools of higher learning in the Arab world (in Cairo and Fes) that are older than any in Europe, but they did not become universities until they were reformed under European influence in modern times. As the name indicates, a university is an institution in which the sum of human knowledge is put on display, and every branch of scientific inquiry finds a legitimate place. It is universal in scope, dedicated to revealing the truth wherever it may be found and to synthesizing it into a coherent whole, a mission that received its first real articulation in medieval Europe.

Some people like to trace the origin of the sciences back to the ancient Greeks, and through them to the Egyptians and Babylonians, but although a case can be made for this, none of those cultures developed what we would call a university. This was because they were unable to define the various disciplines correctly or maintain a balance between them and the principles of coherence that make sense of them in the wider world. Thus we find that mathematics was often seen as something akin to magic and could easily degenerate into numerology, with concepts like perfect numbers coming to dominate it. Astronomy was usually just the handmaid of astrology, a pseudo-science that provided the key to unlock the mystery of the foreordained fate of every individual. History was mainly a branch of ethics, told to illustrate the good and bad deeds of great men whose example was to be emulated or avoided. A few things, like architecture, were studied for themselves, but this was because they had an immediate practical purpose, and they were not regarded as the proper concern of philosophers. Indeed, the thing that stands out most clearly when we look back on it now, is that ancient Greek knowledge was designed for contemplation more than for application. The Greeks knew, or at least some of them believed, that the material world consisted of an almost infinite number of tiny atoms, but it never occurred to them that there was anything they might be able to do with that knowledge. The atoms were there to be imagined, not to be employed, and nobody tried to classify the elements in the way we now do. Even the most sophisticated thinkers never got beyond the basic four – earth, air, fire and water – that were thought to make up the universe, an erroneous belief that stifled scientific progress for centuries.

To make matters worse, the ancients confused material reality with moral and spiritual values. Everything material was evil and only non-material ideas were spiritual, or real. To be intelligent was to escape from the world as much as possible, and the smartest people, the philosophers, were as detached from material reality as they could be. This was not a recipe for scientific progress, with the result that ancient theories remained just that – theories.

Christianity changed all this. Few people now realize it, but the great theologians of the early church wrote commentaries on the creation story in Genesis 1-3 more than on any other part of the Bible, because they understood that it contradicted the fundamental beliefs of their inherited pagan culture and challenged them to replace it with something that was true to reality. The biblical revelation gave a new structure to their universe, rationalizing what had previously been jumbled up and delineating distinct spheres of endeavor that we now think of as academic disciplines. The material world was demythologized and set free for the human mind to study it for what it is. At the same time, moral and spiritual values were also liberated by the creation of the new discipline of theology, which explained mankind's place in the world as the agent of the creator God, whose will could be known and obeyed.

By virtue of their creation, human beings were made in the image and likeness of God, which gave them the capacity to think God's thoughts after Him, to respond to His leading and to act as His agents within the sphere of responsibility allotted to them – the material world. As the creation of the supremely rational mind, this world operates according to principles that we call scientific laws. Human beings have the capacity to work out what those laws are and to use them for the development of the untapped potential that the material order contains. We do not have to sit back in awe at what God has made or be fearful of touching it in case we might disturb its inner workings. On the contrary, we have been given dominion over it, with the right to till the ground, to exploit its resources, and to adapt it in ways that will release its hidden potential. To do this effectively, we must first understand it, and that is what a university is for. In analyzing the created order we define the different scientific disciplines and work out the consequences of the principles that govern them. Furthermore, we are called to treat each aspect of God's creation as valuable and valid in itself and not simply as a means to getting access to some higher spiritual truth. In other words, astronomy and mathematics have their own inner logic and purpose, and are not to be regarded as mere stepping-stones to the supposedly higher art of predicting the future.

The Bible teaches us that creation is the work of a spiritual being, but that it does not reveal spiritual truth to us in and of itself. For that we must go elsewhere, to the revelation, which has been given to us through the prophets and apostles, and supremely in the life, death, and resurrection of Jesus Christ. He is the key to the meaning of the universe, because He is the creator who became a creature in order to show us what the ultimate purpose of our creation is. We are called to rule over the material order, not as an end in itself, but as preparation for a greater assignment awaiting us in heaven. When we die we shall go into the presence of God and sit with him on his throne, ruling the universe with him and according to his will. What we learn in the restricted sphere of earth will be transformed by the expanded horizons of heaven, when the purpose of all things, including our existence, will be made plain. The university is the arena in which we are called to develop knowledge and understanding of the world that has been entrusted to us, but to the Christian mind, a true university is one that goes further and submits that task to the overarching rule of God.

This is why the first universities regarded Christian theology as the queen of the sciences. Theology was meant to inform the scholar about the nature and purpose of his task in the world, helping him to see where his particular piece of the jigsaw puzzle fits in the wider picture. It was not intended to dominate, invade, or censor the other disciplines, but to provide them with coherence and purpose – seeking the mind of God through the mind of man. The modern university has generally rejected this dimension, even in those cases where it retains a theological faculty. The result is that it is a body without a head, a corpus of knowledge without meaning. Those who fought for this kind of secularization believed that in doing so, they were liberating the world from the tyranny of a pseudo-discipline that consisted mainly of mythology which church and state both used to impose morality on the ignorant masses. They thought that if theology could be dethroned the human mind would be free to discover the true nature of reality by the unfettered use of its own rational nature. What they did not understand is that rational inquiry can analyze data but has much more difficulty in following this up with an adequate and persuasive synthesis.

To put it simply, science can tell us how things function the way they do, but not why they exist in the first place or even what they are ultimately for. But the human mind seeks the sort of meaning that only such a synthesis can provide, and if it cannot look to any higher authority, it will try to find what it needs within one or more particular disciplines, thereby distorting our perception of the whole. Thus we see how economists read the world through the eyes of economics, reducing all activity to the needs and trends of the market. Sociologists create their own fantasy world based on their limited observations and analyses. Biologists interpret everything through the lens of Darwinian evolution, even though Darwin never claimed to have discovered a comprehensive explanation of ultimate reality. It does not matter what the discipline is; those who are engaged in it find themselves obliged to use it as a tool for discovering something more fundamental and all-embracing. It is here that Christian higher education can make its contribution, by restoring the divine dimension to academic study and putting the human mind firmly in its place, not in order to diminish it but in order to allow it to be the instrument of learning that it was originally intended to be.

The Contemporary Challenge

Today we live in a world that has experienced a

knowledge explosion. It is true that such things have happened before, most notably in the late fifteenth and sixteenth centuries, when the invention of printing and the discovery of the new world produced a form of globalization that marked the transition from the Middle Ages to the modern world. More recently, the invention of the telegraph, and later of radio and television, made instant access to information a reality and brought home how much we are affected by what goes on in previously remote corners of the earth. However, these information revolutions, important as they were, pale in comparison with the recent expansion of the Internet and related technologies. It is now possible to access almost anything from the computer on your desk and to search it instantly with tools that earlier generations could only have dreamed of. At the same time, it is now possible for anyone to express an opinion about something without being restricted by the judgment of an editor. This means that a frustrated genius living in a backwater can publish his theories without let or hindrance, but it also means that we are stuck with a vast amount of spurious or pseudo-knowledge, spread by cranks who can no longer be controlled.

Nevertheless, that there has been a positive democratization of the learning process cannot be denied. In parts of the world that lack the resources needed to build great libraries, knowledge can now be disseminated at low cost, and a villager working in a hut in central Africa can scale the heights of academe almost as easily as a scholar working in the privileged surroundings of an Ivy League campus.

Globalization brings with it different perspectives which claim a place at the table alongside traditional Western, and essentially Christian, values. These perspectives may be religious, ideological or cultural, but whatever their origin, they often seek to challenge the dominant paradigm of Western civilization, which has made such globalization possible. We in the West have been forced to re-examine our own value systems and consider what their relationship is to ultimate or objective truth. This is not simply a matter of abandoning our traditional perspectives and adopting those of another culture; rather it is asking ourselves how we can see through the constructions our civilization has made and find common ground with those who have a different starting point.

Given the historical relationship between Christianity and Western culture, it is inevitable that Christian values will come under scrutiny in this analysis. Has our religion shaped our culture or been shaped by it? Can Christianity be exported to other societies without westernizing them in the process? Questions like these pop up in endless conferences and seminars, but they all function within the same academic paradigm, which is that of a modern liberal, and basically Western, society. Africans or Indians who complain about being colonized by the West do so in terms borrowed from their colonizers, and they interpret their own heritages in the same way. To take but one example, those who speak about the need to empower Asian women so that they can realize their full potential in the global economy are using a vocabulary and adopting a value system that makes sense only within the context of current Western society. Most of the women who are the intended beneficiaries of this are probably unaware of what the academics are talking about, would not understand it if they were, and might well reject it if it were imposed on them. The rise of Islamic and other fundamentalisms in the developing world are evidence of this, because very often they are fueled by the resentments and incomprehension of those who are being involuntarily confronted by such reasoning.

Closer to home, we experience this kind of thing as the need to encourage diversity and multiculturalism. In reality, these words are used to camouflage a process of homogenization, in which people of different backgrounds are integrated into a social framework that represents a kind of lowest common denominator. The moral and spiritual values of Christianity are co-opted for this project to the extent that they can be, but the essence of our faith is left to one side because it is too exclusive to fit the current politically correct framework. The result is a new form of incoherence, in which socially desirable values like equality and justice are promoted, while inconvenient truths, like the total depravity of the human race and our absolute dependence on the saving grace of God, are dismissed, even though our concepts of equality and justice make no sense without them. This matters, because the world we now live in is one in which people everywhere have bought into the aspects of Western culture that they like without being in tune with the Christian spirit that animates it. As a result, it is not only the fruits of advanced technology, but also the freedom that our legal system is designed to protect, that are taken over and manipulated by fanatical groups and used to further their own ends.

For example, Islamic fundamentalists are allowed to promote their cause in Western countries by using the resources of our media and hiding behind the rights conferred on them by our constitutional provisions, when their only aim is to destroy such things. It seems incredible that such people can be found serving in our armies and have even used their guns to fire on their fellow soldiers, all because weeding them out would be an unacceptable form of discrimination against a minority group. But that is the situation in which we now find ourselves. So detached has our secular value system become from reality that we are committing social suicide in the name of tolerance, and can do nothing about it because the resources we need to combat it come from a religious outlook, which is considered by many to be just as dangerous to our collective well-being as any terrorist threat might be. Is there any way to overcome this blindness and reaffirm the fundamental importance of our faith for the existence and prosperity of the society that it created and has sustained in the past?

The Christian Response

How should Christians respond to the challenges we face today? Can we reclaim a culture that does not share our convictions, or that shares them only to a certain extent? What do we say when confronted by the accusation that we, too, are fundamentalists, demanding a submissive adherence to an irrational belief system that is by definition a brake on progress?

First of all, we must resist the claim that modern secularism is the rational norm by which everything else must be judged. Human reason is a great and wonderful thing, but it is a means to an end and not the end in itself. To mistake the method for the object of our study is to falsify both, because it forces reason to shoulder a burden it was never intended to bear. Science, the product of rational inquiry, can tell us many things about how the universe functions, but it cannot tell us why it exists or what it is ultimately for. We cannot persuade atheistic rationalists to accept the Christian faith, but we can argue that their objectification of reason is false and unable to provide a coherent explanation of reality.

Secondly, while we must let each academic discipline operate according to its own internal principles without interference, we must not let it exceed its remit and seek to become a standard by which everything else must be judged. If a geologist discovers ancient fossils that date back millions of years, the Christian cannot interject that this is impossible because, according to the Bible, the universe was made only six thousand years ago. Such naive misapplications of Scripture are precisely the sort of thing that brand Christians as fundamentalists and make it impossible for believers to gain a hearing in the academic community. There is no contradiction between the biblical evidence and what science has discovered, but how these things interconnect cannot be reduced to a simple literalism that nullifies the evidence. Nothing is more necessary today than deep and responsible thinking about the interface between faith and science, both of which have their place in the mind of God and neither of which can diminish the witness or importance of the other. At the same time, it is equally naive to elevate the principles of biology as revealed by the fossil record into a norm that can explain the origin and purpose of the universe as a whole. Whatever truth there may be in evolutionary theories, they cannot tell us everything, or even very much, about realities outside their own limited sphere, and to think that they can is to succumb to a fundamentalism just as bad as the one Christians are sometimes accused of.

Thirdly, we must insist that the world is a coherent whole that can be examined and understood by minds that have been made for that purpose. We cannot relapse into theories of randomness or meaninglessness that excuse us from having to figure out what the truth is. As Christians we do not deny the existence of mystery, but we affirm that it can and has been known in Jesus Christ. Having a relationship with God, whose thoughts are higher than our thoughts, we should have no problem about rationally accepting things that go beyond our understanding, because that understanding was never intended to exceed the bounds placed on it by our Creator. All human knowledge is finite and relative. Anyone who pretends that he has found the key to solving every problem is not only wrong but dangerous, because in using that key he will inevitably exclude large parts of reality which do not fit into his paradigm and by doing so he will seriously distort what remains.

Fourthly, we have to maintain our commitment to universality. What is true for us is true for everyone. To pretend otherwise is to discriminate against people who have as much right to know the truth as we have. Christianity is not a Western religion but an expression of universal truth that has created and shaped what we call Western culture. It has not been the only influence on that culture, but it has been decisive, and even the rejection of Christian values that is so widespread today is possible only because those values themselves allow it. Nobody is forced into the kingdom of heaven, and we are warned in the New Testament that there will always be many who will be blind to the truth and reject it. We have to go on living with them and respect their freedom to think differently from us, but we cannot sit back and let them exercise hegemonic control over our culture in the name of universal values that are really no more than their own opinions. For example, Scott Brown, a United States senator from Massachusetts, was recently criticized for being insensitive enough to say that it is abnormal for a lesbian couple to have children. The assumption made by Mr. Brown's liberal critics is that there is no real difference between homo- and heterosexuality. But the biological fact of the matter is that two lesbians cannot have children without involving a third party, who may remain anonymous but whose existence is nevertheless essential for children to be produced. It is therefore perfectly correct to say that having children in such a relationship is abnormal. Those who think otherwise have constructed a paradigm of normality that does not correspond to the biological facts. Christians are not trying to impose particular social values when they say this, but to point to an inescapable reality and insist that it, and not some postmodern fantasy, should be the foundation of our public norms. To think otherwise is to degenerate into a new mythology that has taken leave of the truth and can only lead in the end to cultural death.

It is essential for the Christian mind to grasp this, because every society creates its myths, even if it claims to be based on reason alone. Christian theology puts spiritual truth in the place of myth, bringing reason and order to the world beyond our sense perception and explaining how we are connected with it. The relegation of that theology to the sidelines of modern discourse has left a vacuum that fantasy has not been slow to fill. We may employ the resources of psychology and hi-tech, but it is fantasy all the same, and like the mythology of old, it will do nothing but pervert our knowledge and blind us to the realities that we are called to confront and control.

Universality also means that truth transcends cultural boundaries. As Christians we know that we are imperfect, but this is true of others as well. The notion that we should abandon our traditional habits and assumptions in favor of Eastern religious practices that supposedly offer a surer guide to enlightenment is false. Neither Hinduism nor Buddhism possesses a vision of reality in any way comparable to the Christian one. Our understanding may be faulty and our ability to implement it may falter, but these are defects in us, not weaknesses inherent in our faith. We have to approach other faith traditions with respect, but we cannot regard them as viable alternatives to our own. Jesus said that He is the way, the truth and the life, and that no one can come to the Father except through Him. This is a bold claim to make, but if we believe in Christ then we must accept it and put it into practice. To refuse to share the gospel with people of other cultures on the ground that we do not want to interfere with their traditions or think that we are superior to them is to deny Jesus Christ, who is the Lord and Savior of all mankind, not just of the Western world.

Fifthly, we must remember the relativity and inadequacy of our own conceptions and way of thinking. As Christians we can be comfortable with this because we understand that God knows what we do not. We do not sense that we have failed if we cannot find an answer to everything, nor do we try to force our understanding into a pattern that does not fit it. Dominion over the creation was given to the entire human race, not to a single individual or group of individuals. It may be helpful to embrace a certain philosophy or adopt a particular technique to deal with the issues confronting us right now, but we do not canonize these things or imagine that they will serve us well in every circumstance.

For many centuries Christians were content to use Platonic concepts to express their faith, but the inadequacy of these is now understood, and we are less willing to adopt them than our forebears were. In recent times, some people have tried to express their faith in

Marxist, Darwinian, or Freudian categories, but while each of these may have something illuminating to tell us, none of them can be an adequate basis for developing the Christian mind. In the end, our faith is not a philosophy or an ideology, but a relationship with the One who made us and to Whom we owe all that we have and are.

That relationship is rooted and grounded in love, and that love is the essence of the Christian mind. The God who made us has not abandoned us to our own devices, nor allowed us to succumb to our fate. He is a God who loves us because He has made us, and who continues to love us even when we disobey Him and do all we can to get as far away from Him as possible. He comes to us in the depths of our sinfulness and in our deepest despair, when there is nowhere else for us to turn. He does not excuse our disobedience or ignore our rebellion, but He deals with them by sending His only Son to become one of us, to take our burdens on Himself and to die for us, paying the penalty that you and I could never pay, so that we might be restored to new life and put back in the place that He wanted us to dwell in from the beginning. The love of God punishes Himself so that we can be restored to the right relationship with Him. It is a love that binds us to Him and reaches out through us to the world to which we are called to bear witness.

Everything we do, we must do in love if it is to bear any lasting fruit. When we understand this we can begin to see that it is God's love that holds the universe together and constitutes its fundamental being. The secular world pays mock tribute to this by making love its cherished ideal, and yet it does not take much to see that the way love is worked out in our society is a travesty of the real thing.

True love is only possible in and through God,

because only God is truly love. Tom Corts knew this, and dedicated his life to making this vision a reality at Samford University. Such a project can only ever be a work in progress, and he has left us much to do. But he built his legacy on a solid foundation of which his family and friends can be proud and of which we are all the beneficiaries. May God grant us the grace to use that legacy wisely and to further in our own small way the wonderful project that is the kingdom of God on earth.

Editor's Note:

Lyle Dorsett was introduced to Tom on joining Samford University's Beeson Divinity School faculty. Dorsett became better acquainted with Tom when they discovered a mutual love for Christian biography. "We especially talked about the need for biographies of minor figures in American church history," Dorsett said, and "... we agreed to do some writing in this genre, encourage one another in this field of scholarship, and we even contemplated editing a series of minor figure biographies. Indeed, at the time of Tom's death, I was reading a book manuscript he had written on Horatio G. Spafford." Author of eighteen books, Dorsett is the Billy Graham Professor of Evangelism at Samford's Beeson Divinity School.

CHAPTER 4

LIGHT BEARER IN A DARK PLACE:
A PORTRAIT OF
WILLIAM PLUMER JACOBS
(1842-1917)

By Lyle W. Dorsett

When Tom Corts and I first met we discovered a
shared interest in more than our enthusiasm for Christian
higher education. We both loved books, especially
Christian biography. What delighted us even more was
our keen interest in a sub-field of this genre, minor-figure
biographies. Soon after this discover, Corts placed in my
hand a copy of his book on P.P. Bliss with a promise that
he would consider writing a full-scale biography. In the
meantime he wrote a draft of a biography of Horatio G.
Spafford, which certainly merits publication.

Our interest in minor-figure Christian biography
stemmed from a presupposition that reputations of

famous people in history often obliterate lesser-known but extremely important people in God's economy. Bringing these silent but significant historical figures into the spotlight helps enrich our understanding of the past. By showing that the great people of any era do not toil in isolation, the Monet-like impressionistic paintings of history can be complemented by more precise and detailed Rembrandt-like canvases.

A historian and theologian who understood this point of view was J.C. Ryle. In his classic, *The Christian Leaders of the Last Century* (1878), Ryle set forth an indisputable but long-neglected truth that for a hundred years people had known of the roles played by John Wesley and George Whitefield in the English revival of the 1700s. But it was Ryle's thesis that many other "great men were not sufficiently known, and their merit in consequence not sufficiently recognized."[1]

Corts and I agreed that forgotten saints need to be celebrated, not only to enrich our view of the past but to help our contemporaries learn from the lives of important people who never achieved recognition except in their smaller corners of life. Our assumption dovetailed on this and another point. Ordinary Christians, like us, would do well to learn that God's will is to bring glory to Himself through women and men who never achieve fame. Indeed, biographies of such people can also underscore key elements in their lives that made them useful for kingdom purposes.

Tom Corts and I discussed some of the people we thought should become biographical subjects. One man glistened like gold as we panned the sands of late nineteenth and early twentieth century American history, William Plumber Jacobs. So, as a modest attempt to carry on Corts's vision to help build the Kingdom of the Lord

Jesus Christ through the genre of objective Christian biography, I offer this cameo portrait of Jacobs.

****

Although a sketch of William Plumer Jacobs appeared in the early twentieth century *Dictionary of American Biography*, later twentieth century historians largely passed him by in such widely acclaimed works as *A History of Christianity in America* (1992), *Dictionary of Christianity in America* (1990), *Eerdmans's Handbook to Christianity in America* (1983), and *The Biographical Dictionary of Evangelicals* (2003).

To the superficial observer, William P. Jacobs might appear provincial. Born in York County, South Carolina, in 1842, he died less than 100 miles away in Clinton, Laurens County, South Carolina, in 1917. Yet during his lifetime, this native South Carolinian became a far-sighted Presbyterian pastor, educator, author, editor, publisher, and humanitarian who brought glory to God and honor to the label Christian. Indeed, through a life devoted to loving God and serving his impoverished neighbors, William P. Jacobs became a light bearer to a dark part of America devastated by the angry scars of the Civil War and Reconstruction.

With a first-rate mind disciplined by an excellent college and seminary education, Jacobs travelled throughout the United States, Britain, and Western Europe. And for the few people who have been fortunate enough to discover his published *Diary*, or the obscure biography of him written by one of his sons, Jacobs's life inspires and encourages others to this day.[2] A case in point is the late Peter Marshall. Raised poor and fatherless in the industrial heart of Scotland, Marshall migrated to America in 1927 at the age of 24. He graduated from Columbia Theological Seminary in 1931 and eventually served as senior pastor of New York Avenue Presbyterian Church in Washington, D.C., and as chaplain of the U.S Senate. Catherine Marshall, his wife and biographer, made it clear that William P. Jacobs's diary and life encouraged Peter as a young seminarian and nudged him toward a closer personal walk with the Lord Jesus Christ.[3]

William P. Jacobs was born and raised in a privileged environment. Although his father never acquired great wealth, he worked hard to gain a broad liberal arts and theological education, eventually distinguishing himself as a Presbyterian minister and educator. He briefly taught in secondary academies in Alabama and Georgia and then spent most of his career in Charleston, South Carolina.

Young "Willie" Jacobs, as he was affectionately called by his family, lost his mother at a very young age. Although his father remarried a kind woman, the lad bonded most closely to his father who raised him to lead a life of obedience to God, to honor parents and discipline his mind on academic books and the Holy Bible.[4] Encouraged by his father's love for books and the world of nature, young William became an intellectual with a biblical worldview. As he studied philosophy, history, literature, natural science, and mathematics, he also learned Greek, Syriac, German, Hebrew, and Latin. Throughout much of his life, William studied six days a week, and devoted two hours each morning to prayer and reading his Bible in Greek and Hebrew. His early love for the Bible, plus his father's love for Scripture and the liberal arts, caused William to embrace, in the spirit of Psalm 8, a love for all of God's creation, which the Creator had entrusted to the stewardship of man.

At age sixteen, William P. Jacobs claimed Jeremiah 45:5 as his life verse. "Seekest thou great things for thyself? Seek them not." He wrote in his diary, "This is the word of the Lord. O Lord, help me to seek great things not for myself but for Thee. Help me lay all of my laurels, all my learning at Thy feet and help me to look up to Thee as my friend and law giver."[5]

A few days after this journal entry, he admitted it would be a struggle to keep this focus because "I have always been seeking great things for myself. To be honored, loved and respected by all has always been my greatest ambition. I will [instead] seek them for God...I will strive and try not to gain great things for myself but to gain them for God."[6] About a month and a half later the purposive teenager sensed a call from God "to preach His glad tidings of great joy to the world..."[7]

William P. Jacobs proved to be an unusual young man in that he never fell away from pursuing his life verse and calling to preach the gospel. Although his diaries reveal occasional dark nights of the soul – especially when other Christians, including ministers, gossiped, caused divisions, or assaulted his character with no evidence to support their charges – he never lost his way.

On the eve of the Civil War while continuing his studies in Charleston, Jacobs confided, "I have come to the conclusion that slavery at best is a diabolical practice." He also admitted to changing his attitude toward secession. "I was awfully a Secessionist but now I am a strong Unionist. I would not see one quill plucked from the wing of that proud bird which is emblazoned over our Senate hall."[8]

Like Robert E. Lee who loved the Union yet ultimately manifested more loyalty for his home state of Virginia, nineteen-year-old William P. Jacobs pledged his loyalty to South Carolina when she succeeded from the Union on December 24, 1860. This occurred three months before he graduated from the College of Charleston. Unlike General Lee, however, Jacobs never fought for the Confederacy, as his eyes were too weak to pass the physical examination. Instead, he moved to the state capital at Columbia and began studies for ordination in the Presbyterian Church at Columbia Seminary, where he graduated in 1864.

While still a seminarian, Jacobs received a license to preach in Presbyterian churches. Consequently, in 1863 he began serving two small churches in Laurens County near Clinton. Slight of build and standing just 5'6" tall, the student-preacher sported rimless glasses, a Van Dyke beard, and a well-trimmed mustache – all of which conspired to make him look older than his twenty-one years.[9] Jacobs became an ordained minister after graduating from seminary in May 1864. Soon after, he received a call to pastor a little Presbyterian Church in Clinton with the added responsibility of providing services twice a month to two other rural churches within a thirty-minute horseback ride.

Just three months after becoming pastor, Jacobs assisted in organizing a countywide revival. His three little flocks, plus other small congregations in the county, gathered for several evenings of preaching and singing. During one of those meetings Pastor Jacobs looked down from the platform and spotted a lovely twenty-year-old brunette named Mary Dillard. From that moment on, he found it difficult to look at anyone else. He noted in his diary that "Miss Mary D" lived at Coldwater, a Laurens County plantation home just a few miles from Clinton. Over the next few weeks the infatuated preacher made several trips to Coldwater to pay his respects to the young lady. By the end of the January 1865 they had committed their love to one another.[10]

The wedding took place on April 9, 1865 – the same day General Robert E. Lee surrendered at Appomattox. The newly married pastor confessed to his journal, "peace is being discussed. God grant that it may come. The war, however, had not been the principal theme of my thoughts."[11] If the Civil War did not dominate the young pastor's thoughts in April 1865, the effects of four years of fratricidal conflict and post-war Reconstruction affected every part of the Palmetto State's economy, polity, and society. To put a fine point on things, South Carolina, like much of the South, had been devastated by war. It would require decades of rugged determination, hopeful endurance, and otherwise undreamed of human sacrifice to overcome the conflict's crippling effects.

From the time he heard a call to ministry, young Willie had longed for an opportunity to minister in a rural community beyond the Tidewater region of his home state. Convinced now that the Lord Jesus Christ had given him the desires of his heart, as well as a lovely wife for a helpmate, twenty-three-year-old Pastor Jacobs set out on his journey to "show the world what God can do in Clinton, South Carolina."[12]

When Pastor Jacobs arrived in Clinton in 1864 he described it as nothing more than a crossroads – a "village of three years' growth."[13] Numerous promises of prosperity had existed prior to 1861, but war had retarded all growth. By 1864, all able-bodied men had gone to war, their women and children scattered to relatives in rural areas. Slaves found themselves in a morass of uncertainty. With General William T. Sherman's army penetrating the deep South during the last year of the war, reigning fire and destruction on cities like Columbia and Charleston, rural South Carolina became a sea of wandering humanity

– former slaves looking for shelter and field work, urban refugees trying to stay a few miles ahead of thunderous Union armies, and wounded Confederate soldiers limping home after giving their blood and limbs to a lost cause.

There was too much mobility for anyone to compile accurate population statistics. But at war's end, William estimated Clinton's population to be well under 200 people. The village remained stagnant in the following years. By 1872 conditions seemed so grim that some people assumed their town would disappear.[14] As pastor, William expressed both concern and commitment to the fledgling town. In 1871, when a pastor invitation came in from Anderson, he refused, saying, "I cannot leave Clinton."[15]

By all objective measurements, Pastor Jacobs's determination to remain in Clinton became the turning point in the town's history. During the next forty-two years, Clinton gradually recovered and even prospered. By the time of Pastor Jacob's death in 1917, the population had grown to over 5,000 and boasted several permanent institutions. All of these institutions remain in place today, albeit in modified form. All were products of Jacobs's vision, faith, and enterprise. He credited the impetus behind these works to the Lord Jesus Christ, and he underscored that his wife's commitment and labor were absolutely essential in bringing light to a very dark place.

The Reverend Jacobs, although not thirty years old until 1872, manifested wisdom and vision beyond his years. He believed Clinton could not emerge from the ashes of war or become a viable community if everyone wallowed in post-war despair, bemoaning the passing of "the good old days." To his optimistic mind, people needed hope and that hope must first come from God, who could make all things new and redeem the economic devastation.

Consequently, he first invested his energy in building a strong church. To be sure, the young minister was tainted by the segregationist culture of his time, but he had, after all, opposed slavery and it became obvious that he loved the freed slaves as well as the whites. For example, when he first began holding worship services he visited and invited the freedmen, as well as the whites. By the late 1860s his Sunday worship services included blacks and whites from both Clinton proper and from nearby farms in the surrounding rural area.[16]

Apparently, as many "colored," as he labeled them, attended as whites. He even noted in his journals that the freedmen were sometimes more attentive and stirred by his sermons and Bible classes than the white congregants. Given the social mores of Reconstruction, it is certain that the two races were segregated in all services and Sunday school classes, with whites in the front and blacks in the back. Nevertheless, the forward-looking minister showed his concern for the souls of all his parishioners by laboring to construct a church building for the blacks as well as the whites.[17]

It would be wrong to assume William P. Jacobs labored to build facilities and draw crowds as evidence of his success as a pastor. On the contrary, he believed all people were lost and on a path toward eternal damnation without a personal faith in the Lord Jesus Christ to whom they must turn through confession of sin and earnest repentance. Jacobs never exhibited a lust for more numbers. Yet his journals show he maintained a passion for souls, and he continually asked the Lord to give him lost people to serve.[18] Both Pastor Jacobs and his wife Mary shared the conviction that no one could fulfill the Great Commission without also living out the Great Commandment by caring for the whole person. Coming to faith in Christ was the foundation of a God-glorifying life but it was only the beginning.

Mary Jacobs gave birth to five children, four sons and a daughter, between 1866 and 1877. These children were raised to love and fear the Lord, and their parents also sought out a good liberal arts education for them. Both William and Mary enjoyed the privilege of being raised by parents and surrounded by people who treasured the world of the mind as part of the nurture of the soul. Naturally they wanted the same advantage for their children.

To their credit, William and Mary also desired the same educational opportunities they wanted for their children for other children and youth as well. It is out of this Christ-inspired purpose to love their neighbors as themselves that they labored side-by-side to bring educational opportunities to Clinton. It never occurred to the young couple that state or national governments should care for the physical well-being and education of their neighbors. On the contrary, they assumed Christians – and the churches in particular – had a God-given responsibility to feed and clothe the poor and educate the ignorant. To their way of thinking, works of charity and education must be given in Christ's name and for His glory, and the worldview that undergirded the educational system must be biblical.

As a result, William and Mary did much more than build up Clinton's Presbyterian Church; they simultaneously launched several programs that became effective institutions. These efforts would strengthen the town of Clinton and cause it to be a beacon of light during the trying years of the late nineteenth and early twentieth centuries.

South Carolina, like much of the South, found

itself challenged by thousands of homeless children left destitute by the ravages of war. Nearly 134,000 Confederate soldiers died on the battlefields or in hospital wards. Tens of thousands more were left maimed and incapacitated. Such tragic circumstances left many children orphaned. Other boys and girls, although one or two of the parents might actually be alive, found themselves in such dire circumstances that they roamed the countryside, looking for food and some means of livelihood.

Early in their marriage, William and Mary Jacobs determined to alleviate this problem. They committed to educating children in the Clinton area and to providing shelter for those who were homeless. Their joint efforts became evident to everyone. One Clintonian summarized it well, saying, "Mary gave herself totally to whatever work her husband undertook."[19]

The Jacobses ultimately pursued many enterprises together, but the most famous and enduring was the Thornwell Orphanage. Named after Dr. James Henley Thornwell, a professor at Columbia Seminary, as well as a theologian, pastor, and mentor to William Jacobs, the orphanage was inspired by several factors. First, the Holy Bible reveals God's heart for the fatherless. As students of Scripture, William and Mary did not miss God's call to His chosen people to care for the orphans. Second, William read two books that became impetuses behind the orphanage. He read George Mueller's famous work, *A Life of Trust*, and from it learned how God had enabled Mueller and his wife to house, feed, clothe, educate, and introduce to Jesus Christ thousands of street urchins in industrial England during the middle 1800s. Mueller's book not only tells the story of a great work for God's glory, it reveals that people who pray with faith can find all necessary support for such work. Mueller never asked anyone but God for money. Amazingly the needs of thousands of orphans were met.[20]

Jacobs also found inspiration from a volume written about Immanuel Wichern who established an orphanage for boys in Hamburg, Germany, in 1832. What particularly caught Jacobs's attention in Wichern's ministry was his conviction that too much institutionalization would exacerbate the lack of human interaction and love that already plagued the orphans. Instead of a large impersonal institutional building with a dormitory and big dining hall, Wichern opened small houses with no more than a dozen boys assigned to each place. In an earnest attempt to create a home-like environment, housemothers oversaw each house and each facility had its own kitchen. Meals were cooked in the house and the boys and their housemother ate together family style.[21]

Mary and William imitated what they could from both Mueller's and Wichern's models, and then they embarked upon a journey of faith to care for as many children as possible. At the outset they urged the Presbyterian Church to join them in opening the orphanage. Although the church embraced their venture and encouraged people to support it, it did not send funding. In fact, many years would pass before the Presbyterians contributed financially to the orphanage.

Pastor Jacobs became known as America's George Mueller, at least in the southeastern United States. Whatever the image, the work required much personal sacrifice. To pursue a vision like Mueller's might sound glamorous in vision, but in reality it was quite the opposite. Finding funds to construct and maintain each cottage became a challenge, as did maintaining the buildings once they were constructed. Money came in, thanks to the beneficence of philanthropist Nettie McCormick, wife of Chicago manufacturer Cyrus H. McCormick, who supported the work for twenty years. Funding also came from some generous South Carolinians, as well as a continual stream of small donations from countless ordinary individuals. Consequently, the first specially designed orphan cottage was opened in 1875 with eight children. Its ministry continued unabated until Pastor Jacobs's death. Ultimately, fourteen buildings were erected, including an infirmary, school, library, and enough houses to accommodate as many as 300 children. By the time William died in 1917, more than 3,000 children and youth had been cared for and many went on to live lives that brought glory to God and honor to Thornwell Orphanage. For example, of the 14 lads who lived in Faith Cottage in 1881 and 1882, four became ministers, one a foreign missionary, and one a physician.[22]

In addition to fundraising, William and Mary took on the arduous task of finding suitable "house mothers" for each cottage. Some women proved to be incompetent; others were gossips. Eventually the couple made the difficult decision to make their home the "first stop" in order to meet the immediate needs of the incoming orphans and to demonstrate that they truly believed in the work. All the while William remained pastor of the church at a salary of $600 a year, an amount he seldom received in full. More than once he was paid with worthless Confederate dollars; often his pay came in the form of chickens and corn.[23]

The demands of the orphanage, church, and five children took its toll on Mary Jacobs's health. Despite the fact that almost none of the pastor's salary was paid in 1878, some Laurens County pastors and newspaper editors accused the Jacobses of conducting their ministry for money. Mary died from the stress of slander and overwork on January 16, 1879.[24]

The couple's vision for Clinton encompassed more than housing, feeding, and clothing orphans. It included providing a Christian liberal arts education. Both Mary and William believed children's minds needed nurturing every bit as much as their hearts and souls. Although Mary helped plant the first seedlings of liberal education, she did not live to see the fruit. Before her death, formal co-educational classes were held for the orphans. But eventually separate girls and boys' academies were formed. Before his passing in 1917, Reverend Jacobs lived to see the development of fully functioning elementary and secondary schools and, with the help of the Presbyterian Church, an intellectually respectable and educationally challenging four-year Christian institution called Presbyterian College.

Always a hopeful and energetic man, William P. Jacobs expanded his vision beyond an orphanage, schools, and college for Clinton. He secured a printing press that eventually produced several periodicals. While his first publishing ventures were short-lived, they paved the way for future works. He launched a four-page weekly, *The True Witness*, in 1866 that lasted only a year but went on a year later to publish *Our Monthly For the Fireside, Farm and Garden*. After wisely shortening the title to *Our Monthly*, it became a fairly successful 68-page periodical replete with educational articles and news about the Orphanage. Jacobs also edited the *Phonographic Quarterly*, which promulgated his zeal for phonography (stenography and short hand).

The energy of this intellectual maverick knew few boundaries. William went on to open a small natural history museum, featuring a splendid mineral rock collection originally gathered by his father and a rare coin collection. Always the educator as well as a pastor, Jacobs used both collections to interest students in geology and numismatics. Additionally, William constructed the first two-story house in Clinton as a sign of his faith in the community's permanence and opened the first community library.

An avid reader from childhood, William began collecting books as a young man in Charleston. Eventually he assembled a personal library of more than 3,000 volumes, which he said, "have become in part a history of myself." The collection consisted of a set called The Sacred Classics, the writings of William Gilmore Simms, the Waverly novels, church history, ancient history, British and American history, philosophy, biography, several U.S. state histories, and several periodical sets, including *The Southern Presbyterian Review*, and other valuable volumes of theology that had belonged to his mentor, Dr. Thornwell.[25]

Despite all of these enterprises, Pastor Jacobs never neglected his church ministry. His diary entries abound with prayers to the Lord for the salvation of souls, and he continually asked God to bring more spiritually lost people to his church. He preached regularly, taught Bible classes, and manifested a heavy burden for Clinton's black population. "I am laboring among the colored people, sowing seed that I hope to see someday grow into good harvest. The colored praying meeting is going well."[26]

His work among the former slaves is remarkable. Laurens County became a hotbed of Ku Klux Klan activity in the early 1870s. That Pastor Jacobs risked censure despite the widespread anti-black sentiment gave him credibility with these marginalized former bondsmen and women.

Such manifestations of love notwithstanding, Jacobs

was far from flawless and proved to be chained to the racism of his times. He never fell out of sympathy with the Ku Klux Klan, although he hated all their violent behavior. He saw jailed Ku Kluxers as a persecuted group, and he allegedly made comments about a Jewish man visiting from New York that can only be seen as horribly anti-Semitic.[27] In short, he was a white Southerner of his times, though his passions and prejudices were tempered by his faith.

William P. Jacobs was mightily used by God despite imperfections was nowhere more evident than his relationship with his spouse. To be sure his diaries reveal a deep devotion to her. And it is true that Mary loved him unstintingly and worked with him in all church and orphanage endeavors. Yet his diaries and journals reveal that Mary's health was less than robust. Even during their months of courtship she was often confined to house and bed. Despite her apparent frailty, this petite wife and mother labored sacrificially to support the church, orphanage, and her family. William never confided to his diary that Mary's efforts might be harmful to her health. In August 1873 he recorded, "Mary and I have concluded to offer our house and ourselves to the Thornwell Orphanage. God only know where this will lead to. This makes the way clear to opening the Orphanage immediately. I am anxious for the building of the Orphanage."[28]

They gave themselves to the orphanage to be sure. By turning their house into the first orphan's home in 1873, Mary became de facto housemother to eight homeless children. This was burdensome enough, as she already had four of her own children under the age of seven, with the fifth and youngest being only five weeks old. She gave birth to a sixth child in 1877. Perhaps she fully shared her husband's enthusiasm for this donation "of our house and ourselves" at this particular time. Regardless, her grandson's research revealed that six years later, by 1879, she carried a load impossible for her constitution to bear. He wrote, "Due in part to her duties involved in caring for some twenty-five children, Mrs. Jacobs died in 1879."[29]

William's obsession with the Presbyterian Church and the orphanage, plus his drive and determination to create a liberal arts educational environment, revealed both his strengths and his weaknesses. Perhaps some of the difficulties he experienced in finding and keeping good housemothers and teachers, as well as his controversies with local pastors and townspeople, stemmed at least in part from his unusually high expectations for what ordinary people could do.

In the final analysis, the life and ministry of William P. Jacobs mirrors an important theme. God calls imperfect people to lead His chosen people and build His Kingdom. Despite Pastor Jacobs's flaws, God used him to raise up a strong church, care for hundreds of homeless children, and to bring an organized system of Christian liberal arts education from elementary through college level to a people blinded by ignorance. Jacobs also helped blacks and whites take early steps toward racial reconciliation, and he became a promoter of economic opportunity, assisting in acquiring two railroads, a cotton mill, and numerous other enterprises for Clinton and Laurens County.

What factors account for the way he ultimately brought glory to God and light to his community? First of all, William P. Jacobs was a man with a single eye. He called it his "fixed principle." He lived out as best he could the exhortation from Jeremiah 45:5: "Seekest thou great things for thyself? Seek them not." His diaries, published letters and talks, as well as the recollections of family and associates, reveal that Jacobs tried to apply what he preached. He stayed in Clinton despite the difficult times and sometimes strong opposition to his work. At least five times he turned down offers to assume pastorates that would have provided much more prestige and financial security. Furthermore, he never asked others to do things he would not do himself, including the plowing and planting of acres of land to feed the children.

Despite numerous bouts with spiritual depression, Jacobs never lost faith in God's gracious sovereign plan to work all things together for His glory and the ultimate good of those who love Him. Concomitant with this, Jacobs managed to stay hopeful, always manifesting a positive spirit. He refused to look back at "the good old days" of antebellum South Carolina, but instead pushed forward, determined to show the world that God could glorify Himself in Clinton. The diaries make it clear that he sustained his ministry by setting aside time every day to be in "the secret place" with Jesus Christ. There he read his Bible, reading through the entire Old and New Testaments every year, and he talked to the Lord, poured out his needs, and listened to Him in prayer.

Foundational to this remarkable man's life of faithful witness and ministry was his trust in and intimacy with the Lord Jesus Christ. One of his grandsons, Hugh Jacobs, summed it up well in an address at a Thornwell Founders Day. "Christ was as real to Dr. Jacobs as one of the persons with whom he ate and talked, and everything that he did he enjoyed, because he did it for someone else, and because he did it with Christ."[30]

William Plumer Jacobs stayed faithful and busy to the end. On Sunday, September 9, 1917, this aging man with failing eyesight preached twice and then visited the orphans. Early on Monday morning he complained of a headache and prayed that the Lord would take him home before he became totally blind. Within a few minutes after the prayer, at twenty-to-six in the morning, the seventy-five-year-old minister's lamp went out. He finished quietly and well.[31]

References:

[1] J.C. Ryle, *The Christian Leaders of the Last Century* London: T. Nelson and Sons, 1878), iii

[2] Thornwell Jacobs, ed., *Diary of William Plumer Jacobs* (Oglethorpe University: Oglethorpe University Press, 1937); Thornwell Jacobs, ed., *William Plumer Jacobs Memorabilia: Literary and Biographical* (Oglethorpe University: Oglethorpe University Press, 1942); Thornwell Jacobs, *The Life of William Plumber Jacobs* (New York: Fleming H. Revell, 1918).

[3] I corresponded with Catherine Marshall in the early 1980s about Jacobs and some other men whose writings profoundly influenced Peter Marshall. See the "Sermons and Prayers" section at the end of Catherine Marshall's book, *A Man Called Peter: the Story of Peter Marshall* (New York: McGraw-Hill, 1951). Note the sermon titled "Sin in the Present Tense" and the reference to Jacobs's journals and biography on page 304.

[4] This and the following paragraphs comprise summaries of data contained in the three books cited in Note #2.

[5] Thornwell Jacobs, *Diary*, 37.

6   Ibid., 37-38.

7   Ibid., 40.

8   Thornwell Jacobs, *The Life of W.P. Jacobs,* 51.

9   See plate of photos facing p. 212 in Jacobs, *Life of Jacobs.*

10   Thornwell Jacobs, *Diary,* 114-119.

11   Ibid., 122.

12   Thornwell Jacobs, *Life of Jacobs,* 92.

13   Thornwell Jacobs, *Diary,* 112.

14   Thornwell Jacobs, *Life of Jacobs,* chapter 9; *Diary,* see years 1865-1872.

15   Thornwell Jacobs, *Life of Jacobs,* 89.

16   The generalizations in this and succeeding pages come from reading Jacobs' diaries and his son's biography.

17   Thornwell Jacobs, *Life of Jacobs,* 86.

18   For example, see Ibid., 72.

19   This quotation comes from an article titled "Thornwell: A Profile of Love". The author's name is not mentioned. The text is in the archives of the Library at Presbyterian College.

20   Thornwell Jacobs, *Life of Jacobs,* 101.

21   See William P. Jacobs, III, Unpublished manuscript titled "William Plumber Jacobs: Minister and Humanitarian," in the archives of the Presbyterian College Library, 5.

22   "Thornwell: A Profile of Love," 45.

23   Thornwell Jacobs, *Memorabilia,* 622.

[24] Thornwell Jacobs, *Life of Jacobs*, 140; Thornwell Jacobs, *Memorabilia*, 623.

[25] In the late 1980s I was able to examine his personal library in the Special Collections of the Presbyterian College Library. See also Jacobs's own comments on his library in Thornwell Jacobs, *Life of Jacobs*, 249.

[26] Thornwell Jacobs, *Diary*, 164.

[27] Thornwell Jacobs, *Memorabilia*, 604; *Diary*, 164.

[28] Thornwell Jacobs, *Diary*, 163, 164.

[29] William P. Jacobs, III, "William Plumber Jacobs: Minister and Humanitarian," typescript in the Library, Presbyterian College.

[30] Thornwell Jacobs, *Memorabilia*, 623.

[31] Thornwell Jacobs, *Life of Jacobs*, 252; Thornwell Jacobs, *Memorabilia*, 484.

Editor's Note:

Following an exceptional career as an award-winning history faculty member at Auburn University, Wayne Flynt is now Professor Emeritus at Auburn and continues his active civic service, serving as editor-in-chief of the history section for the online Encyclopedia of Alabama. Tom and Wayne bonded on a Christian's responsibility to engage in public service. Tom served with Wayne on the Board of the Alabama Poverty Project, which Wayne formed and Tom vigorously supported, and also on the board of Alabama Citizens for Constitutional Reform, which Tom led and Wayne supported. Wayne was also a founding member of the Samford University Board of Overseers.

CHAPTER 5

THE CHRISTIAN SCHOLAR AS PUBLIC INTELLECTUAL: THE STRUGGLE FOR JUSTICE IN ALABAMA

By Wayne Flynt

The Informal Education of a Christian Scholar

The intersection of Christian discipleship, intellectual engagement, and public policy is one of the most contentious venues of faith. The Christ-against-culture crowd avoid the meeting place as if it were the devil's own holy ground. Those who emphasize personal piety and private spirituality believe no good can come from such conflicted turf as well.

Other Christians on both left and right relish the site. Anthony Campolo, long-time chair of the sociology department at Eastern College in St. Davids, Pennsylvania, and Jim Wallis, founder of Sojourners magazine, visit the intersection regularly. Daring to reject America's three most pervasive ideologies – materialism, hedonism, and narcissism – they relentlessly challenge both secularism and Christian amnesia about social and economic injustice.[1] On the right, Richard Land, Jerry Falwell, and Pat Robertson mobilized Christian scholarship on behalf of public policy designed to end abortion, prevent homosexual marriages, and inject religion into the public square.

All participants in this debate cite Scripture as the source of their activism or rejection of it. Both Old and New Testaments reverberate with God's thunderous calls for justice for His people. But some perceive justice as a matter of private morality while others see it as an issue of public morality. Of the hundreds of passages pertinent to the debate, Isaiah 10:1-3 encapsulates the arguments best: "Woe to those who make unjust laws, to those who issue oppressive decrees to deprive the poor of their rights and withhold justice from the oppressed of my people, making widows their prey and robbing the fatherless. What will you do on the day of reckoning, when disaster comes from afar? To whom will you run for help? Where will you leave your riches?"

When I first met Tom Corts, I had no idea where on the Christian continuum – from pietistic disengagement to activist liberal or conservative engagement – he might be found. With a full agenda of problems to solve as president of a major American university, he might have avoided the public square altogether. And in the early years of his tenure, he did stay pretty close to home. This did not surprise me. With a classics degree from Indiana University, a conservative and nominally Republican ideological bent, administrative experience at a variety of colleges, long residence in Indiana, Kentucky, and North Carolina, a young family to raise, and a complex university to run, no one expected much more of him.

Yet, from the inception of the Alabama Poverty Project (APP) in the early 1990s, Tom demonstrated sustained interest. He not only agreed to serve on the board, he actually attended meetings, provided office space and a part-time faculty position in sociology, and made insightful suggestions. He devised a fundraising strategy. The idea of a non-partisan, faith-based organization such as APP, devoted to dispelling myths about poverty, educating the public, mobilizing churches on behalf of justice for the poor, and engaging Alabama's academic community in the effort caught fire with him. About the same time, Tom offered Samford as a host to the non-partisan Public Affairs Research Council of Alabama (PARCA) and helped persuade Jim Williams to become its first director. Within years, PARCA had established itself as the state's premier public policy think tank.

Next, Tom accepted chairmanship of Alabama Citizens for Constitutional Reform. Convinced that the state's convoluted 1901 Constitution had institutionalized the state's social, racial, educational, and economic injustice, he concluded that the best hope for substantive improvements in the lives of the poorest, blackest, and least powerful Alabamians depended on structural constitutional changes. This intellectual and spiritual pilgrimage carried Tom into a new religious dimension of life, away from the insularity and sanctuary of a small college campus and into the rough and tumble world of Alabama politics. Over a period of two decades, he became a keen student of the state's history. More than all but a handful of state leaders, he fully grasped not only the presence of injustice but its historical sources as well.

Sowing the Whirlwind: A Look Back at Alabama's History

The nexus Tom discovered at the core of injustice involved race, class, greed, flawed educational and tax policy, the 1901 Constitution, and politics. As an intellectual with little initial knowledge of Alabama, he worked backward from symptoms to sickness. Alabama's system of public education was obviously broken. The state's citizens paid the nation's lowest taxes and derived the fewest benefits. Public health was a scandal. Racial attitudes polarized the citizenry into warring camps. Economic development constantly improved based on the state's own checkered past but trailed more progressive Southern states. Weak ethics laws and lack of enforcement invited public corruption. Tutored by former governor Albert Brewer, who taught both Alabama history at Samford and in the university's Cumberland Law School, and by PARCA's Jim Williams, Tom began to connect current injustice to bygone decisions, actions, and policies.

During antebellum times, Alabama law prohibited teaching African Americans (who by 1860 constituted nearly half the population) to read and write. The state provided no schools for black children. Black adults could not vote. Many white ministers and their congregants considered blacks to be a sub-species of the human race, and they justified their racism by quoting Scripture. Without the moral underpinnings of their biblical rationalization of human bondage, slavery would not have endured as long, some European countries had already banned it by 1861, or precipitated a bloody civil war to end it.

On the other hand, the state's antebellum tax system was amazingly fair in the way it derived public revenue. Buoyed by the political power of yeoman farmers and craftsmen, the legislature levied the heaviest taxes on those who owned the most land, slaves, and luxury items. Taxes were low because few expected that the state would provide better services. In fact, the legislature did not even establish a statewide system of public schools until 1854.

Rebuilding the state after the cataclysm of the Civil War placed new demands on government, complicated by massive changes brought about by federal laws and new economic realities. Two of the three legs on which tax policy had rested collapsed; land values plummeted and slavery was abolished. The freedom and enfranchisement of nearly half the population who were illiterate not only thrust them into the state's political system with a fierce desire for education and expanded economic opportunity but also terrified white landowners who would have to foot the bill for additional state services.

Between 1860 and 1874, taxes not only tripled but engulfed the smallest landowner. Between 1860 and 1870, the typical value per acre of a 160-acre farm declined by one third while the tax on that same farm increased by two-and-a-half times.[2] Especially in the Black Belt – where most African Americans lived, most cotton was grown, and most black public officials were elected – whites bitterly resented both black political power and escalating taxes levied by them and their white Republican allies. This resentment coalesced in 1874 into the Redeemer (or Bourbon) movement. Officially naming themselves Conservative Democrats, leaders of the movement used white resentment of higher taxes, racism, violence, and intimidation to re-impose white rule and bring Reconstruction to an end.

The institutional structure of this reaction took form in the 1875 Constitution. Fearful of openly disfranchising black voters lest federal authorities intervene, conservative Democrats limited their capacity to tax property by establishing maximum rates both statewide and in counties. These provisions not only capped state, county, and city property taxes, they also decentralized education and assured its chronic under funding. The Conservative Democratic party thus positioned itself in opposition to Republicanism, advocating reduced expenditures for state services and lower taxes, cessation of government subsidies for private industries, white supremacy and racial segregation, and traditional values as opposed to social experimentation. Conservative elites might not be able to convince working-class whites that they shared the same class interests but they could win a hearing by portraying themselves as champions of white racial solidarity and extolling the virtues of low taxes.[3]

This racial alliance of elite and ordinary whites held until the 1890s, though it was already fraying a decade earlier due to growing economic and political unrest among white yeoman farmers and industrial workers as their economic circumstances grew steadily worse. By the 1890s, insurgent white reformers, allied to hill country and Wiregrass Republicans and blacks, launched a full-scale rebellion against the Conservative Democratic party. This insurgency threatened to topple conservative white rule and was only contained by chicanery, intimidation, vote stealing, violence, and racial demagoguery.

Shaken both by the extent of white class-based revolt in the 1890s and the specter of continuing black neo-Reconstructionism, conservative white planters and businessmen conspired in 1901 to contain these threats with a new Constitution. Ostensibly promoted as a way to end political corruption, improve school funding, and eliminate black voters, the subterranean agenda of the constitutional delegates was to protect their property from higher taxes. All 155 delegates to the convention were white males, mostly lawyers and bankers.

Both the campaigns to elect delegates to the constitutional convention and ratify their proceedings pivoted on racial arguments. The conservative state press left no doubt that ratification of the new document constituted a struggle between whites and blacks for supremacy. On November 5, 1901, the Montgomery Advertiser editorialized that "all white people who have studied it [the proposed constitution] and who are not carried awry by prejudice will vote for it." The *Birmingham Age-Herald* on that same day admonished voters, "Vote then for a white supremacy that does not involve dishonest elections. Vote for the new Constitution." The following day the same paper reminded voters, "What is most wanted for the general good is assured white supremacy." The *Choctaw Advocate* in southwestern Alabama editorialized on November 6, "This is the time when all white men should stand together. The new Constitution was made by white men, for white men." The Democrats Ratification Campaign Committee adopted the slogan "White supremacy! Honest elections! And the New Constitution! One and inseparable."

Ratification passed by a vote of 102,000 to 82,000, but failed statewide except for the returns in twelve Black Belt counties. Each of the twelve contained a majority of black voters, who, despite its provisions for disfranchising them, approved the new constitution overwhelmingly according to the official ballot count. Most of those same counties had also recorded heavy majorities against the biracial populist insurgency that had threatened to defeat Conservative Democrats in 1892 and 1894 gubernatorial contests.

In addition to striking almost all black males from the state's voting lists, the new Constitution essentially adopted the caps on property taxes included in the 1875 document. As a consequence of the 1901 Constitution, few blacks were permitted to vote until the passage of the Voting Rights Act in August 1965. Black historian Horace Mann Bond notes the unequal competition between whites and blacks to divert tax monies to their respective schools after 1901, a contest which blacks stood no chance of winning. As a consequence, white schools statewide, especially in the Black Belt, were funded at many times the per capita rate of black schools. Bond notes:

> In the financing of the general school system this 'obsolete' taxing machinery continued to emphasize property values. As a result, expenditures for Negro children were directly connected with direct land taxes; and any expansion of facilities for Negro children had to meet the full brunt of the old opposition of the 'taxpayers' versus the non-taxpayers and left the Negro population totally at the tender mercies of the white population where almost every conceivable grant of privilege or citizenship was concerned . . . . After 1901, the development of Negro schools was even more than ever at the mercy of stark social and economic influences, divorced of any ameliorating effect which the exercises of the franchise may have introduced in the past. For many reasons, therefore, the Constitutional Convention of 1901 is the definite climax of the problem of educating Negroes at public expense.[4]

The Brookings Institution evaluation was less wordy. "The policy of limiting taxation in Alabama has proved defective, detrimental, and unsound."[5]

Reaping the Whirlwind

Beginning with the Brown vs. Topeka, Kansas, Board of Education Supreme Court decision (1954), both federal courts and Congress began to dismantle the South's system of racial segregation. By the following decade, a series of federal court rulings and Civil Rights laws threatened the historic hegemony over blacks that whites had exercised for nearly a century. Rapidly changing events put them under siege on many fronts, especially in the Black Belt: the declining total population of the Black Belt, threatening the region's control of the legislature; even more rapid decline of the region's white population, threatening white control of local county government; massive registration of black voters; the election of blacks to local offices, including the strategic positions of tax assessor and state legislator; the potential that black county officials would raise county property taxes in order to increase educational opportunities; the exodus of whites from public schools, which created dual public-private systems divided by race; court threats to reapportion the legislature and enforce uniform tax assessment.

In May 1969, the Fifth Circuit Court of Appeals struck down Louisiana's "Freedom-of-Choice" method of maintaining segregated schools. During the ensuing 1970 session of the legislature, lawmakers passed a private school grant-in-aid act, which paid private school tuition for white children whose parents refused to send them to integrated schools. The following year, 1971, U.S. Federal Judge Frank M. Johnson ruled in the Weissinger case that Alabama's assessment of property values varied so greatly as to be inequitable and constitute a violation of the 1901 Constitution, which required that property be assessed at

100% of fair market value. In 1967, the real property tax rate was 17%.

Legislating for Special Advantage

Panicked legislators, especially in the Black Belt, interpreted these interlocking events in apocalyptic terms. In their political eschatology, the end of the world could not be far off. While they might be fatalistic Calvinists in theory, they were passionate political activists in fact, determined to change the outcome of events.

In 1967, the Alabama Farm Bureau Federation (AFB) backed Bill 502, which established the maximum property tax rate at 30% of real value. Four years later, AFB introduced a "classification" system, which lumped property into one of three categories for purposes of taxation: utilities (highest), general property, agricultural/residential (lowest). At first the Farm Bureau listed residential property in a higher classification than farm land, but House majority leader Rankin Fite warned that if the bill was viewed by the public as merely a tax shelter for farmers, it stood no chance of passing.

Under intense pressure from a public that was anti-tax to begin with, urban and education forces in the legislature fought a rear guard action to block the classification system, also called "lid bill" for placing a ceiling on property taxes, and current use. Under current use legislation, a piece of land was taxed based on how it was currently used rather than on its actual market value; in this way, owners of a 104-acre plot in Mobile County adjacent to I-65 and a major mall, and valued at $13.4 million, paid $147.29 in county property taxes in 1990 after it was classified as "forest land." Three legislative enactments – in 1972, 1978, and 1982 – sponsored by the Farm Bureau, the Cattlemen's Association, and the Forestry Association put in place a system that essentially removed a town or county's ability to reassess and tax property at a rate adequate to fund decent public services for its citizens.

No one at the time doubted the authorship of these bills. The *Montgomery Advertiser* editorialized on July 16, 1972, that the "forest products and corporate farm interests so intent on passing the lid bill have been riding too long on a property tax discount ticket at the poorer Alabamian's expense." The *Birmingham News* wrote on December 6, 1971, "For the sake of the majority of Alabama's ad valorem property tax payers we hope the Senate is not eager to have the Alabama Farm Bureau's classified tax reform bill railroaded through that chamber as it was through the House . . . ." The paper noted that Governor George Wallace was quarterbacking the measure through the legislature on behalf of his rural white allies. The fingerprints of the same rural legislative coalition were all over the 1978 and 1982 measures.

There are two ways to view this pivotal legislative moment in Alabama history. One is through the lens of the modern anti-tax movement. All Americans hate taxes. They particularly resent paying taxes if they believe their money is being wasted. As the nation's most conservative, anti-tax state, one should look no further than to understand what happened in Alabama.

An alternative explanation begins with an opaque field of vision, obscured by race. It had been blacks and their white Republican allies who had nearly tripled property taxes during Reconstruction. And this "waste" of tax dollars on black schools still rankled with many whites. Since whites paid most property taxes and increasingly sent their children to private, segregated academies by the 1970s, why should they pay higher property taxes in order to educate Negro children in nearly all-black public schools?

The most compelling argument for the latter interpretation is historical context. Segregation was under siege during the three decades from 1954 to 1984. No blacks served in the legislature until 1970, when two were elected to the House from the Black Belt. Almost every subsequent election cycle added to their numbers until blacks constituted one quarter of the legislature by 1993, enough to block property tax caps by filibuster. Furthermore, reapportionment broke the back of Black Belt control of government. The Voting Rights Act increased the percentage of eligible black voters from a little over 20% to more than 50% in four years' time. Local black officials began to raise property taxes. By the 1970 Democratic gubernatorial primary, when George Wallace ran the most racist runoff campaign in Alabama history, Black Belt whites believed their backs were against the wall.

Fortunately for the planter regime, they had just enough time left, sufficient legislative experience, and the forceful advocacy of Governor Wallace (himself a Black Belt power broker from Barbour County) to insert protection of their economic interests into Alabama's 1901 Constitution. But the Farm Bureau left its racial fingerprints all over their handiwork.

Senator Walter Givhan of Dallas County became the Bureau's chief legislative sponsor of the 1972 and 1978 bills. Born into a Perry County planter family, Givhan by the 1940s owned a large plantation near Safford in western Dallas County. Farmers elected him president of the Dallas County chapter of the Farm Bureau in 1942. During a three-decade career in both houses of the legislature, he became the principal legislative spokesman for the Bureau. Governor John Patterson identified him as the most effective representative of anti-tax interests as chairman of the powerful Senate Finance and Taxation Committee.

In October 1947, Givhan verbally attacked populist Governor James E. Folsom at the annual Farm Bureau state meeting. According to Givhan, Folsom and his advisors were following a "Red" [Communist] course. "Every Negro in Alabama . . . voted for Folsom . . . It is time for the farmers of Alabama . . . to declare themselves. The extreme leftists, or Reds, are going about trying to dominate us and they will, unless the farmers do their part."[6]

Givhan certainly played his part in preventing the tax-and-spend Reds from taking control of Alabama. In an August 4, 1948, letter to segregationist leader Sid Smyer, he described blacks as "uneducated masses" who were unqualified to vote. "The trend in Alabama . . . is towards turning our government over to the masses, and in my opinion if we do not place restrictions and qualifications on a voter at this session of the legislature, we will have seen our last election in Alabama where the people who carry the burden of taxation would have any voice in our state government. This is our last chance, if we turn the ballot box over to the uneducated masses in this State we can expect nothing but chaos . . . ."[7] Writing fellow segregationist leader Gessner McCorvey on January 29, 1949, Givhan returned to the same theme. "We must do something to protect Alabama from the mass registration of Negroes which is about to take place; and which if allowed to happen, will destroy democracy in Alabama government as you and I have always known it."[8]

As white racial sentiment hardened following the Brown decision, Givhan was elected chairman of the Dallas

County White Citizens' Council (1957-58), which among its other activities had Negroes fired who tried to register and threatened white ministers whom they concluded were insufficiently firm segregationists. From 1958 until 1962, Givhan served as chairman of the state White Citizens' Council. He spoke frequently at Citizens' Council meetings, ranting that the real goal of the NAACP was "to open the bedroom doors of our white women to Negro men." "This is a white man's country," he continued; "it always has been and always will be."[9]

In 1964, he warned that the public accommodations bill passed by Congress "threatens to make all our freedoms null and void and to destroy our present American way of life." Speaking in Selma, Givhan credited the withdrawal of federal troops from Little Rock to the efforts of the Citizens' Councils. "We will always be on top, and eventually we are going to win a complete victory in our fight to preserve our sacred way of life."[10]

Under Givhan's leadership, the Dallas County Citizens' Council became the state's largest, helped form chapters in adjacent Black Belt counties, and was selected as the top council in America at the 1961 national Citizens' Councils Convention. In October 1962, Givhan and other Dallas County Council members flew to Oxford, Mississippi, as an advanced party to help block James Meredith's integration of the University of Mississippi. Appalled to discover black soldiers at the airport, he wired Alabama's congressional delegation. "You cannot conceive of the tragedy which has befallen your native land. Please come immediately to Oxford and see for yourself the gravity of the threat which our democratic form of government now faces."[11] During Alabama's massive resistance campaign, Governor Wallace appointed Givhan to the segregationist State Sovereignty Commission, whose task it was to document the communist ties and sexual excesses of Civil Rights leaders.[12]

In Dallas County, Givhan led the movement to fund segregationist Morgan Academy. He also sponsored a bill for farm tax exemptions in August 1970, the same session of the state senate that enacted a private school grant-in-aid plan to pay the tuition of white children unwilling to attend integrated schools, for which he voted. On July 18, 1975, Givhan wrote J.D. Hays, president of Alabama Farm Bureau, that he was appalled at the growing influence of the Alabama Education Association (AEA), which opposed the Bureau's various attempts to limit property taxes for public schools. He deplored a bill just passed by the legislature that allowed teachers to deduct AEA dues from their salaries, calling it "the beginning of unionizing all the teachers in Alabama." Givhan continued, "Unless this trend slows down . . . they may be able to have enough power in the future to remove our [tax] exemptions."[13]

Nor was Givhan alone in his role as white, Black Belt defender of segregation and low taxes. Representative Joe McCorquodale of Clarke County, who served as Speaker of the House during the 1978 lid bill and 1982 current use debates, owned real estate and agricultural lands valued at more than a million dollars and earned more than $10,000 from the sale of timber during 1981 alone, according to an April 29, 1982, article in the *Birmingham News*. Rick Manley of Demopolis in Marengo County, another key Farm Bureau leader pushing property tax limitations, sponsored the 1977-78 lid bill in the House and introduced the current use bill in the 1981 session. Farm Bureau lobbyist John Dorrill wrote McCorquodale on May 31, 1981, that without his assistance and Manley's, "the land owners would have never been able to enjoy the benefits of classification, the lid bill, and now current use."[14]

The final actor in this legislative drama was James Deford Hays, president of Alabama Farm Bureau during the 1970s and 1980s debates over property tax limitations. Hays came from a large plantation family in Haysland, south of Huntsville, was a founding director of Compass Bank, as well as longtime president of AFB. His extensive correspondence files reflect the economic and racial ethos of the Black Belt more than the progressive economic development strategies and racial openness of Huntsville during these decades.

Hays' identification with segregationist politics permeates Farm Bureau records and his papers. He introduced George Wallace when the governor addressed the October 1963 annual Farm Bureau state convention. Hays began his introduction with an admonition to President John F. Kennedy, declaring, "Down here in Alabama, you are not as big a man as you are in Massachusetts." He then announced that he had invited arch segregationist Mississippi U.S. Senator James Eastland to address the convention. When Eastland suddenly cancelled, Hays asked Wallace to substitute.

Wallace began his speech with a tribute to Eastland. "I wish we had more Senators like Senator Eastland; the country would be a lot better off than it is." The remark drew loud applause from Farm Bureau members. Wallace claimed that majority white and black football teams in Philadelphia could not play each other because of violent racial incidents. He then verbally assaulted Attorney General Robert Kennedy, attacked "liberal Birmingham newspapers," other media, and "outside agitators," and proposed cracking down on Aid to Families with Dependent Children and other "welfare cheats" – all to roars of applause from his audience. He criticized the use of military bases in the South to bring about social and racial changes, called the Public Accommodations Act unenforceable absent creation of a police state, and warned that the Justice Department would dictate to hotels who could sleep in their rooms and tell hair dressers whose hair they could work on. Next would come land reform for racial compensation, leading to the confiscation of white family farms. The real agenda of the federal government was the destruction of free enterprise and the capitalist system as well as the nation's liberty and freedom. Recently, he alleged, sixteen Communists had met in Birmingham churches to foment racial conflict. His pledge "to send those Kennedys back to Massachusetts" drew the loudest cheers of the evening. The federal government cultivated "left-wingers and bloc voters" and spent so much time supervising state voting registrars that officials had insufficient time to weed out Communists. He urged his listeners to support private academies in Tuskegee and Birmingham before concluding, "I am proud that the Alabama Farm Bureau Federation stands up for freedom . . . and honors me tonight."[15]

Hays invited Wallace to address the annual convention again in 1970, following the governor's racist Democratic runoff victory over Albert Brewer and just before Givhan introduced a property tax limitation amendment in the senate. Wallace urged Farm Bureau to organize state politics as thoroughly as possible. He promised to oppose new taxes and speak out on all national issues. He condemned news media for misrepresenting Alabamians as racists. But he drew loudest applause when he assured Bureau members that "you represent the majority of people in this country." Wallace then recounted his victories for Alabama. He had forced President Richard Nixon to support neighborhood schools and oppose school busing to achieve racial balance;

he had compelled winning congressmen from both parties to endorse his position on school integration and opposition to tax increases. "We will continue to stand up for Alabama," he proclaimed, "and the Farm Bureau of Alabama has stood up for those principles of the majority of Americans."[16]

Following one of Wallace's speeches to Farm Bureau members, John Dorrill, Jr. – who became legislative lobbyist for Alabama Farm Bureau in 1961, later Hays' assistant, and Executive Director in 1978 – closed the evening with an enthusiastic endorsement of Wallace. Dorrill stated, ("Now anything else we could say tonight would be an anticlimax") and promised to do everything Farm Bureau could to assist the governor.[17]

The year after Wallace's inflammatory 1970 speech, Hays invited Lieutenant Governor Jere Beasley to speak at the 50th anniversary convention of Alabama Farm Bureau. Like Wallace, a native of the Black Belt's Barbour County, Beasley told members that the most important issue facing the legislature was the property tax limitation introduced by Farm Bureau in the special session. He predicted that the bill would pass due to the hard work of Senator Givhan, who Beasley as presiding officer of the senate had selected to manage the bill.[18]

Nor did Hays' opposition to federal intrusion into states' rights soften. He campaigned nationally for Wallace among farm groups. On May 5, 1975, he wrote U.S. Senator James Allen, protesting that Alabama was one of only five states still under federal jurisdiction of the 1965 Voting Rights Act. He called such restriction by the federal government "discriminatory and without justification."[19]

Sour Home, Alabama

Describing a century of agricultural change in the state, historian Harvey Jackson noted the rapid decline of farms in Alabama from 200,000 in 1950 to less than 50,000 by the 1980s. As the farm population plummeted, the average size of farms dramatically increased, transforming family farms into agribusinesses. He then summarized the political implications of this transition. "Reacting to this trend, and benefitting from it, the old Farm Bureau transformed itself into the Alabama Farmers Federation (ALFA), shifted its focus to selling insurance, and became a household name in the state," said Jackson. "But ALFA executives still were Bourbons at heart, so with the money they made they hired lobbyists, and with the help of the Alabama Forestry Commission, they did what their Bourbon ancestors had done – kept property taxes low and social services starved."[20]

Jackson could have added another paragraph to his story. Despite its stout defense of conservative values, free markets, the free enterprise system, and its denunciation of federal intrusion and regulations, ALFA officials grew rich off federal agricultural subsidies, used their political influence to write legislation fixing higher insurance rates for non-Alabama based companies (thus assuring ALFA a price advantage on insurance policies it wrote), and protected landed wealth from a fair system of taxation.

Jackson's conclusions express the nearly perfect symmetry at the intersection of tax, race, constitutional, economic, and political change between 1865 and 2000. Reconstruction-era empowerment of African Americans resulted in tripling Alabama property taxes between 1860 and 1875. The violent reaction of large white property owners, especially in the Black Belt where black voting majorities taxed their property in order to fund schools for all children, led directly to the Redeemer ("Bourbon") victory in the 1874 gubernatorial election and the 1875 Constitution, which for the first time, set caps on property taxes. The biracial Populist uprising of the 1890s once again threatened Bourbon hegemony and racial apartheid, resulting in the 1901 Constitution, which maintained the 1875 limitations of property taxes within the context of a rigidly racist document. From that moment forward the conservative faction within the Democratic party (and after the 1960s within the burgeoning Republican party) fiercely fought for a century reformist elements to protect low property taxes and to transfer any additional revenue proposals to sales taxes or other sources.

After the 1954 Brown decision, these same political elites lived in terror of enfranchised black majorities in Black Belt counties that might gain political control and increase property taxes in order to fund expanded social services, especially for schools, as had happened in the same counties during the decade between 1865 and 1875. Federally imposed reapportionment of the legislature during the 1960s, together with successful suits to compel uniform assessment and collection of property taxes early in the 1970s, added new layers of danger to the 1965 Voting Rights Act. So did election of the first black legislators.

All of these threats occurring within a decade of each other created an apocalyptic sense of urgency to limiting taxes on property owned by wealthy whites before invidious federal courts or politically empowered blacks could raise county taxes to improve public schools, which whites were abandoning anyway, or filibuster tax caps in the legislature. Alabama Farm Bureau's long association with the racial views of Black Belt planters and its immense political power in the legislature, until it began to diminish in the 1980s and 1990s, led to the classification system for taxing property, the lid bill, and current use legislation.

Realizing that the racial landscape was rapidly changing, Farm Bureau leaders, like their idol George Wallace, transitioned from the overt racist rhetoric of the 1960s to the covert racial policies of the 1970s and 1980s. As legislative leader and lobbyist, Joe Fine explained in a 2010 deposition that Wallace by the 1970s "had code words that he used. He was a master of touching the nerves. . . . Question: 'Words like federal judges and federal courts and interventions?' Answer: 'Well, he did all that. But in 1970 . . . it was a little more pointed than that. Don't turn it over to them, don't let them take it away from us. . . .'" When asked if school integration was a significant issue in the 1970s, Fine responded that it was, that the state's population was racially polarized, with terms such as "black vote" serving as code words.[21]

The lid bill, classification, and current use debates may not have featured specifically racist language such as characterized public debates in Alabama between 1954 and 1970. Such language would have infuriated and alienated black legislators after 1970 as well as their urban white allies, thus making passage of property tax limitations more difficult. But the policies were no less race-driven.

The preceding century of racial and political conflict, and especially the previous fifteen years of racial upheaval, provide convincing historical context for most Alabama historians. Resistance to the threat of black political empowerment and federal court intrusion continued the racial and economic inequities that had plagued Alabama since Reconstruction, channeled through the most obvious political conduit, Alabama

Farm Bureau, which was the logical successor to the post-Reconstruction Bourbon Black Belt political regime that had ruled Alabama most of the time since 1874. Worse yet, they embedded these inequities in the 1901 Constitution and the state's tax statutes that crippled the state for more than a century thereafter.

References

1   For representative scholarship on the topic of justice, secularism, and Christian engagement, see Anthony Compolo, *A Reasonable Faith: Responding to Secularism* (Waco, Texas: Word Books, 1983) and *We have met the enemy, and they are partly right* (Waco: Jarrell, 1985); Jim Wallis, The Soul of Politics (New York: The New Press, 1994), and *Who Speaks for God? An Alternative to the Religious Right – A New Politics of Compassion, Community, and Civility* (New York City: Delacorte Press, 1996). For an Alabama application of these issues, see Susan Pace Hamill, *The Least of These* (Sweet Water Press, 2003).

2   Wayne Flynt and Keith Ward, "Taxes, Taxes, Taxes," *Alabama Heritage* (Spring 1992), 11.

3   Malcolm McMillan, *Constitutional Development in Alabama, 1798-1901: A Study in Politics, the Negro, and Sectionalism* (Chapel Hill: University of North Carolina Press, 1955), pp. 177, 185-186, 206, 211, 213, 218; Horace Mann Bond, *Negro Education in Alabama: A Study in Cotton and Steel* (Tuscaloosa: University of Alabama Press, 1994 edition), 135-138.

4   Bond, pp. 193-194.

5   Quoted in Bond, p. 193.

6   Quoted in Bill Barnard, *Dixiecrats and Democrats: Alabama Politics, 1942-1950* (Tuscaloosa: University of Alabama Press, 1974), pp. 90-91.

7   Walter Givhan to Sid Smyer, August 4, 1948, Governor Frank M. Dixon Papers, Alabama State Archives. Hereafter, Dixon Papers.

8   Walter Givhan to Gessner McCorvey, January 29, 1949, Dixon Papers.

9   Quoted by J. Mills Thornton in *Dividing Lines: Municipal Politics and the Struggle for Civil Rights in Montgomery, Birmingham, and Selma* (Tuscaloosa: University of Alabama Press, 2002), 401.

10   Ibid., 402.

11   Ibid., 412-413.

12   Jeff Frederick, *Stand Up for Alabama: Governor George Wallace* (Tuscaloosa: University of Alabama Press, 2007), 277.

13   Walter Givhan to J.D. Hays, July 18, 1975, J.D. Hays Papers, Auburn University Archives. Hereafter Hays Papers.

14   John Dorrill to Joe McCorquodale, May 13, 1981, in "Current Use Correspondence," Record Group 543, Accession No. 04-013, Box 22, File 22-2, Farm Bureau Papers, Auburn University Archives. Hereafter Farm Bureau Papers.

15   Audio tapes of speeches in Accession 1980, Box 15, Farm Bureau Papers.

16   Ibid.

17   Ibid.

18   Ibid.

19   J.D. Hayes to Senator James Allen, May 5, 1975, Hays Papers.

20   Harvey H. Jackson, III, *Inside Alabama: A Personal History of My State* (Tuscaloosa: University of Alabama Press, 2004), 277.

21   Deposition with Joe Fine, Lynch case.

Editor's Note:

The creation of the divinity school and chapel at Samford was one of my brother's most gratifying projects. A man of careful reflection, Tom thought long and hard about virtually every detail as the project unfolded. Securing the right leader for the school was a paramount concern for Tom and the subject of intense prayerful meditation and careful research. Tom settled on Timothy George, who was serving as a church history professor at Southern Baptist Theological Seminary at the time. George has modeled scholarship, written extensively, and provided exceptional leadership for the divinity school's development. Along the way, the two men became friends on several levels, including their shared love of classics and ancient history. George pays tribute to Tom by providing this chapter on the great Christian intellectual, Desiderius Erasmus.

CHAPTER 6

THE ERASMIAN MOMENT

By Timothy George

*It is I, as cannot be denied, who have aroused
the study of languages and good letters. I
have brought academic theology, too much
subjected to sophistic contrivances, back to
the sources of the holy books and the study of
the ancient orthodox authors; I have exerted
myself to awaken a world slumbering in
pharisaic ceremonies to true piety.[1]*
Desiderius Erasmus

The life of Desiderius Erasmus (1466-1536)
straddled, almost evenly, the fifteenth and sixteenth
centuries. More than anyone else in his age, Erasmus
embodied the ideals of biblical humanism. At the same
time, he represented the tensions inherent in both the
Renaissance and Reformation. Born the illegitimate son

of a Dutch priest, Erasmus always seemed to be running away from something—from his murky past, from warring popes and imperial armies, from iconoclastic Protestants and stuck-in-the-mud Catholics, from dirty inns with their flea-bitten beds, from bad cooks with their suppers of moldy wine and smelly fish he could not stomach, and always, always from the recurring plague which had carried away both of his parents.

This essay on Erasmus is part of a larger book I have written, *Reading Scripture with the Reformers* (Downers Grove: InterVarsity Press, 2011). I am pleased for it to be published here in a volume meant to honor the life and legacy of my friend and colleague, the late Thomas E. Corts. I first met Tom Corts in 1988 when he invited me to become the founding dean of Beeson Divinity School, an evangelical, interdenominational graduate school of theology at Samford University. In the course of developing this new model of theological education, Tom and I became friends and worked together on many projects related to Christian higher education and the renewal of the evangelical church.

In addition to the establishment of Beeson Divinity School, Tom also promoted a new Department of Classics in the Samford University Faculty of Arts and Sciences, directed from its inception by Stephen R. Todd. The modern study of the classics in a Christian context derives in no small measure from Desiderius Erasmus. It is appropriate that a volume dedicated to the memory of Tom Corts include an essay on the great scholar-educator of the sixteenth century. Like Erasmus, Corts was trained in the classics, was a consummate bibliophile, and strove earnestly to bring together the love of learning and the desire for God.

Erasmus was always a man on the move. He once

said that he had the most learned horse in the world because he had ridden him to all the universities of Europe searching for manuscripts. His books, he said, were his children and "my home is where I have my library."[2] Despite the vast literature devoted to the prince of the humanists, Erasmus remains an enigma. An expert in dissimulation and self-promotion, one wants to ask with many of his contemporaries: "Will the real Erasmus please stand up?" Luther found him as slippery as an eel that only Christ could catch.[3] He had a point.

Nonetheless, there is a common theme running through the twists and turns of Erasmus's long and interesting life. He called it the *philosophia Christi*: a program of educational and moral reform for both the individual and society based on the recovery of classical letters and biblical wisdom and centered around personal devotion to Jesus. At the heart of this philosophy was a disdain for things external. This is how he put it in his 1505 treatise, *Enchiridion Militis Christiani* (The Handbook of the Christian Soldier):

> Do not tell me therefore that charity
> consists in being frequently in church,
> in prostrating oneself before signs
> of the saints, in burning tapers, in
> repeating such and such a number
> of prayers. God has no need of this.
> Paul defines love as: To edify one's
> neighbor, to lead all to become
> members of the same body, to consider
> all one in Christ, to rejoice concerning
> a brother's good fortune in the Lord
> just as concerning your own, to heal his
> hurt just as your own.[4]

In his early years, Erasmus had had jaded experiences with both monasticism and scholasticism, and he was withering in his criticism of both, sometimes attacking the "monks and the theologians" in the same breath.[5] With an eye to his own past, Erasmus said that in the monasteries "men with heaven-sent gifts and born for better things were often buried by ceremonies."[6]

And, recalling his own days as a student of scholastic theology at the University of Paris, Erasmus compared his teachers there to Epimenides, a character of Greek legend who fell asleep in a cave for forty-seven years, although (unlike his professors) Epimenides did eventually wake up![7] Despite many such comments, Erasmus never renounced his own monastic vows, though he did get a papal dispensation that exempted him from wearing the ornate habit of his order, the Augustinian canons regular. He was also exempted from residing in his home monastery at Steyn in Holland. This allowed him to travel at will and become the kind of freelance celebrity scholar known to everyone. On the scholastic front, he did not refuse a Doctor of Divinity degree when it was offered to him (with no coursework and no residence requirements) by the University of Turin. Not exactly a Th.D. from Paris, but at least he was Dr. Erasmus.

Although he spent many hours in his books, Erasmus was no antiquarian. His "philosophy of Christ" aimed for practical and social results. His scholarship was always in the service of the church, though his vision of the church was not limited to the Roman hierarchy from which, nonetheless, he was never willing to separate. A pacifist in an age of war and violence, and an ecumenist in a time of confessional hostility and division, Erasmus tried to apply the principles of peace and love to the fractious world in which he lived. Through erudition and persuasion he aimed for Christian unity and moral betterment. One of his young admirers referred to Erasmus as "the first author in this age of the rebirth of theology."[8] He was also the first public intellectual of early modern times.

Jerome and the Fathers

Basel was a medium-sized city of some 12,000 in the early sixteenth century, larger than its Swiss neighbors, Zurich and Bern, but half the size of Strasbourg and Nuremberg. However, Basel was both a university town and the center of a thriving, international book trade. Here, in 1516, Johann Froben, the greatest printer north of the Alps, brought out two major publications, both landmarks of Erasmian humanism: Erasmus' *Novum Instrumentum*, the first critical edition of the Greek New Testament ever published, and the nine-volume *Opera Omnia of St. Jerome*, which included four folio volumes of the saint's letters carefully edited by Erasmus.[9]

Erasmus had long been a champion of St. Jerome, going back to his school days in Holland when he studied with the Brethren of the Common Life, an order of lay teachers known for their devotion to the great scholar-translator of the early church. The Basel edition of Jerome's works was part of a larger project begun by Johannes Amerbach, Froben's predecessor, to publish new critical editions of the four principal teachers of the Latin Church. Ambrose came out in 1492, followed by Augustine in 1506. Work on the Jerome edition had already begun when Erasmus arrived in Basel in 1514 to become the general editor of the project. He would eventually see Cyprian through the Froben press in 1520.

Erasmus had lectured on Jerome at Cambridge prior to coming to Basel, where the tedious work of collating ancient manuscripts and ferreting out the correct readings accelerated. He complained that he had put more work into reading Jerome's letters than the saint had exerted in writing them.

> Often too I had to work with volumes which it was no easy business to read, the forms of the script being either obscured by decay and neglect, or half eaten away and mutilated by worm and beetle, or written in the fashion of Goths or Lombards, so that even to learn the letter-forms, I had to go back to school; not to mention for the moment that the actual task of detecting, of smelling out as it were, anything that does not sound like a true and genuine reading. This requires a man in my opinion who is well informed, quick-witted, and alert. But on top of this, far the most difficult thing is either to conjecture from corruptions of different kinds which the author wrote, or to guess the original reading on the basis of such fragments and vestiges of the shapes of the script as may survive.[10]

This was the hard labor of textual criticism which Erasmus had learned while serving as an apprentice in the print shop-cum-research institute run by Aldo Manuzio in Venice, the greatest publisher of classical texts in Europe. The same kind of intensive labors Erasmus exerted on the Jerome edition he would expend on the collected works of other fathers of the early church: Cyprian (1520), Arnobius (1522), Hilary of Poitiers (1523), Irenaeus

(1526), Ambrose and Athanasius (1527), Augustine (1528-29), John Chrysostom (1530), Basil the Great (1532), and Origen (1536). Next to Jerome, Origen was Erasmus's favorite church father. The Origen edition was Erasmus's swan song, released just two months after his funeral in the Basel Cathedral.

Reading Scripture with the church fathers was part of the ecumenical bequest of Erasmus to the church of the sixteenth century. Protestant and Catholic scholars alike appealed to the patristic tradition to corroborate their interpretations of the Bible, and to defend their positions in the widening church disputes. Erasmus proceeded on the assumption that if only the writings of the church fathers could be made available in good reliable editions, with the accretions and corruptions of the text cleared away, and the faulty interpretations of the scholastics brushed aside, then serious scholars would be led by the best minds of the early church to the pure teaching of Holy Scripture. Alas, it was not to be. Erasmus bequeathed patrology to the Reformation, but rather than producing an armistice between the warring parties, better editions of the church fathers merely extended the battlefield. Only in recent years, through scholarly projects such as the *Ancient Christian Commentary on Scripture*, have both evangelical and Catholic heirs of the Reformation struggles found a common meeting place in the writings of the early church. Still, the groundwork for this development was laid during the Reformation itself by Erasmus and those who followed him, providing an accessible library of patristic sources.

Luther once said that the main difference between him and Erasmus was that he gave "pride of place to the doctor of grace" while Erasmus preferred Jerome over Augustine. On the crucial doctrine of justification by faith, which Luther called "the head and cornerstone which alone constitutes the church of God," Luther had to admit that not even Augustine had followed St. Paul as closely as he should have. "Let me not put my trust in Augustine – let us listen to the Scriptures."[11] But still, by Luther's lights, Jerome had missed far more in Paul than Augustine because he read law where he should have seen gospel. Yet even Jerome contained golden nuggets worth retrieving. Thus Luther found in Jerome this "really splendid" statement which seemed to corroborate his own view: "The believer does not live because of righteousness but the righteous person lives because of faith, and this means that he does not believe because of his righteousness but is righteous because of faith."[12]

The fact that the major patristic writings were available for the first time in published form during the lifetime of the reformers meant that their exegetical writings were interlaced with citations from the church fathers. For example, in his 1535 *Commentary on Galatians*, Luther quoted many patristic and scholastic writers and carried on a running dialogue with Augustine and Jerome, always to the detriment of the latter.

An old genre, the patristic anthology, appeared in a new form in the sixteenth century. Anthony N. S. Lane has identified some eighty different anthologies that were published in several hundred different editions down to the year 1566. Most of these were produced by Protestant scholars and were organized in a variety of ways reflecting different interpretive patterns and diverse ways of studying the Bible. Some anthologies contained extracts from a single father on a variety of topics. Others covered a number of early Christian writers on ethical topics and doctrinal issues. Still others offered comments on a particular book or section of the Scriptures. Some of the anthologies also included selections by medieval writers such as Bernard of Clairvaux and Thomas Aquinas. Most of these source collections were published in Latin but some appeared in vernaculars, including one in German by Andreas Musculus, and another in French by the Flemish reformer Guy de Brès.

Such collections served two purposes. In an age when scholarly books were still relatively expensive, these handy anthologies made available a library of patristic comment to ordinary pastors and theological students, most of whom could not afford to purchase the multi-volume sets produced by Erasmus and others. Further, by connecting Reformation exegesis to patristic tradition, the Protestant anthologists provided a counterweight to the charge that the reformers were purveyors of novelty in religion. On the contrary, they asserted, if the fathers came back to life today, they would surely be no less persecuted by the Roman authorities than the Protestants were. Luther, Melanchthon, Zwingli, Bucer, Occolampadius, Bullinger, Capito, Peter Martyr – these were the true successors of the church fathers, not the Roman party, which venerated their names but did not follow their doctrine.[13] For all their claiming of the fathers, however, the anthologists warned against their undue exaltation. Their writings should always be judged by the touchstone of Holy Scripture, a standard the fathers themselves heartily approved.

Thus for the Protestant reformers, the fathers were important if subsidiary authorities. In the context of the English Reformation, Bishop John Jewel in *A Treatise of the Holy Scriptures* (1570) spoke of the ancient Christian writers with the kind of critical reverence that was to mark the Protestant theological tradition as a whole:

They be interpreters of the Word of God.

They were learned men, and learned fathers;
the instruments of the mercy of God, and
vessels full of grace. We despise them not;
we reverence them, and give thanks unto
God for them. They were witnesses unto
the truth; they were worthy pillars and
ornaments in the church of God. Yet may
they not be compared with the Word of God.
We may not build upon them: we may not
make them the foundation and warrant of
our conscience: we may not put our trust in
them. Our trust is in the name of the Lord
... I weigh them not as holy and canonical
scriptures. Cyprian was a doctor of the
church, yet he was deceived: Augustine was
a doctor of the church, yet he wrote a book
of Retractations; he acknowledged that he
was deceived . . . . They are our fathers, but
not fathers unto God; they are the stars,
fair, and beautiful, and bright; yet they are
not the sun. They bear witness of the light,
they are not the light. Christ is the Son of
Righteousness; Christ is the Light which
lighteth every man that cometh into this
world. His word is the Word of Truth.[14]

Jerome's Dream

It is not hard to see why Erasmus saw himself
as a new Jerome come back to life again, *Hieronymus
redivivus.* Jerome was the patron saint of sacred letters. In
his preface to the works of Jerome, Erasmus called him
eloquent, a great linguist, knowledgeable in the classics

and history, adept in the study of Holy Scripture – all items that might have come from Erasmus's own curriculum vitae. Like Jerome, Erasmus had also gone through his own "conversion" from classical literature to sacred letters. The tension between these two poles was a persistent theme in his life and work.

Erasmus was well acquainted with the famous story of Jerome's dream in which Christ had confronted the newly converted classicist about his inordinate love for secular writers such as Cicero and Vergil. He much preferred these grand authors to the uncouth style of the biblical writers. He could hardly put down their books in order to pray. Eugene F. Rice recounts Jerome's appearance before an angry Christ in his dream:

> One night, during Lent (probably in 374), when his body was so weakened by fever that death seemed near, he was suddenly caught up in the spirit, *subito raptus in spiritu.* He dreamed that he was called before the supreme Judge. "What condition of man are you?" asked Christ the Judge. "I am a Christian," replied Jerome. "You lie," thundered the Judge. "*Ciceronianus es, non Christianus:* you are a Ciceronian, a disciple of Cicero, not a Christian. Where your treasure is, there your heart is also." The Judge ordered him to be flogged. Smarting from the blows and even more from the burning of his own conscience, he cried out, "Have pity, Lord, have pity." Even the bystanders now fell on their knees and asked the Judge to forgive Jerome's youthful errors and allow him to do penance. Jerome himself swore a solemn oath: "Lord, if ever

again I possess worldly books, if ever again I read them, I shall have denied you." He woke up, his eyes wet with tears and his shoulders bruised and swollen from the divine chastisement, clear physical evidence of the objective reality of his experience.[15]

What has Athens to do with Jerusalem? Or the Church with the Academy? What has Horace to do with Paul? Or Cicero with the Gospels? Can one be both a Ciceronian and a Christian? Such questions had been asked by Tertullian even before Jerome was born. Indeed, the tension between Christianity and classical culture is inherent in the very words of Jesus Himself, which do not come to us in his mother tongue of Aramaic (with few exceptions such as the familial term of address for God, "*Abba*," Mark 14:36, and his cry of dereliction from the cross, "*Eli, Eli, lema sabachthani,*" Matthew 27:46). The Gospels, along with the entire New Testament, were written in the common idiom of Hellenistic Greek. Paul warned against the allurements of vain philosophy, but he also quoted the Greek poets at will and argued with the rhetorical skill of a Quintilian.

Neither Jerome nor Erasmus could leave the classics alone. On his first visit to England in 1499, Erasmus was charmed by John Colet and heard him lecture on Paul's letters at Oxford. The two maintained a close personal friendship until Colet's death in 1519. Erasmus resonated with Colet's piety and his rejection of scholastic methods, but he could not accept his counsel to abstain from reading pagan literature. In his *Lectures on Corinthians*, Colet warned, "Those books alone ought to be read in which there is a salutary flavor of Christ, in which Christ is set forth for us to feast upon. Those books in which Christ is not found are but a table of devils. Do not become readers of philosophers, companions of devils. In the choice and well-stored table of Holy Scripture all things are contained that belong to the truth."[16]

Erasmus knew that Jerome, despite his dream, continued to quote from pagan authors and that Augustine too had recommended such literature for Christians to read. But why study the Greek and Latin classics? Erasmus answered: in order to better understand the meaning of the Bible itself. Drawing on an analogy used by Augustine in the *On Christian Doctrine*, Erasmus asserted that just as the children of Israel carried with them the "spoils of the Egyptians" when they left their land of captivity, so too Christian scholars today may "steal" the riches of pagan learning in order to adorn the temple of the Lord.[17]

In other words, classical literature can and should be appropriated for Christian purposes. This became an important plank in the program of biblical humanism as well as in the Protestant approach to the study of the Bible. Thus when twenty-one-year old Philip Melanchthon came to the University of Wittenberg in 1518, his teaching assignment included the Greek classics (starting with Plato and Homer) as well as New Testament Greek. Just so, when Luther found himself sequestered in the Castle of Coburg during the Diet of Augsburg in 1530, he translated the Book of Ezekiel from Hebrew to German in the morning and the fables of Aesop from Greek to German in the afternoon: the winged seraphim and the tortoise and the hare on the same day.[18]

Despite his enthusiasm for Jerome, however, Erasmus fell far behind his hero in one crucial aspect of sacred learning. While Jerome was the greatest Hebrew scholar of the early church, surpassing even Origen,

Erasmus considered Hebrew too strange and difficult for him to learn and only "nibbled" at the language.[19] Colet once urged Erasmus to lecture on the Pentateuch and the Book of Isaiah at Oxford, but he declined, acknowledging his lack of Hebrew learning. Eventually Erasmus did publish commentaries on eleven of the psalms, although they are more sermonic than textual or exegetical in style.[20]

With other humanist scholars, Erasmus defended Reuchlin against his detractors who not only defamed the greatest Hebraist in Europe but also tried to destroy Jewish writings. Erasmus also continued to push for the ideal of trilingual education in the study of the Scriptures, but his own expertise in only two of the three sacred tongues left him less than fully sympathetic to the study of the Old Testament.

Wolfgang Capito, a reformer in both Basel and Strasbourg, was an outstanding scholar of Hebrew who published a Hebrew grammar (1525) and wrote commentaries on Habakkuk, Hosea, and Genesis. As part of the humanist brain trust in Basel, he assisted Erasmus on textual matters related to Hebrew when the critical edition of the Greek New Testament was being prepared for the press in 1516.

In that same year, Capito, together with Konrad Pelikan and Sebastian Munster, brought out the first edition of the Hebrew Psalter printed north of the Alps. While appreciative of the help Capito had given him, Erasmus spoke slightingly of his devotion to "the Hebrew truth." In words not meant for publication but laced with anti-Semitic sentiment, he wrote:

> I wish you were more intent on Greek rather than on those Hebrew studies, although I do not reprehend them. I see that that race

is full of the most inane fables and succeeds
only in bringing forth a kind of fog . . . I
wish the Christian church did not give such
weight to the Old Testament! It was given for
a time only and consists of shadows, yet it is
almost preferred to Christian writings.[21]

The reluctance of a middle-aged scholar to learn a
new language does not fully explain Erasmus's relegation
of Hebrew to the place of third rank among the three
holy tongues, nor his degrading comments about the
Jews and their language. Some scholars have found in this
attitude a sign of his favor toward a Hellenic rather than a
Hebraic worldview. With his bent toward Platonism with its
disparagement of the earthly and the physical, he found
New Testament piety more congenial than Old Testament
history. As the debates of the Reformation heated up,
Erasmus kept looking over his shoulder at the group of
first-rate Hebrew scholars Luther had gathered around
him in Wittenberg—his "Sanhedrin," Luther called it—
and he seems to have postulated a guilt by association
theory of Reformation origins.
    Luther's positive approach to the Jews in his early
career (as opposed to his brutal attacks on them later)
made Erasmus suspicious of Jewish collusion in the
Reformation tumults. From his base at Basel, Erasmus
could hear the violent noises of the Peasants War across
the Rhine in southern Germany. While he deplored
the savage conflict, he could not help passing on the
rumor that the upheaval had been instigated by the Jews.
Erasmus's exchange with Capito before all hell broke loose
points to a scholarly pattern that would emerge among
his humanist disciples who embraced the Reformation:
devotion to the Erasmian way with respect to the New

Testament and Greek, but for a warmer embrace of the first three-fourths of the Bible than their master could affirm.

The Greek New Testament

In the summer of 1504, Erasmus found himself in the library of the Premonstratensian Abbey of Parc near Louvain. He was doing what he always did in such places: rummaging through the collection, searching in the corners, hunting for some unknown book or long-forgotten manuscript. "In no forest is hunting a greater delight," he once said of such pursuits.[22] This time he struck gold for he stumbled upon a manuscript of Lorenzo Valla's annotations on the Greek New Testament. Valla died in 1457, in the early dawn of the age of printing, and his controversial work correcting the Latin Vulgate by comparison with the Greek original had never been published. Erasmus seized the manuscript, presumably with the permission of the abbot, and carried it with him to Paris where he saw it through the press in March 1505. He appended a preface of his own, justifying Valla's approach to the sacred text and signaling his own desire to make the Bible the primary focus of his own scholarship.

For the next ten years Erasmus immersed himself in the study of Greek. He perfected his text critical skills, scoured older manuscripts of the Bible that came into his hands, and began his own Latin translation of the New Testament. The result was the *Novum Instrumentum* published by Froben in 1516. Erasmus later complained that this first edition had been rushed into print, "precipitated rather than edited," for fear that someone else would beat him to the punch.[23] In fact, we now know what the publisher Froben perhaps surmised: that the New Testament had already been printed in Greek in 1514 as part of the Complutensian Polyglot in Spain. But this edition would only be published after 1520 when the entire polyglot project received papal approval. Aware of the defects in the 1516 edition, Erasmus began at once to work on a second revised edition which came out in 1519 and which he called more familiarly, *Novum Testamentum.* The process of clarifying textual variants, acquiring better manuscripts, and improving his Latin translation proved to be an ongoing task. Eventually Erasmus brought out five editions of the Greek New Testament during his life, in 1516, in 1519, in 1522, in 1527, and in 1535.

To cite just one of the embarrassing gaffes that Erasmus had to correct in later editions: the last five verses of the Book of Revelation had been omitted by the copyist Erasmus had hired to prepare the final transcription of the text for the printer in 1516. In haste to see the project through the press, Erasmus promptly and extemporaneously translated the missing verses back into Greek from the Latin. He had always claimed, with Jerome, that a translator was the servant of the inspired text, not a conduit of fresh revelations. Erasmus's ad hoc solution to the problem of the missing verses, while showing his facility with Greek, betrayed his own philological principles and added unnecessary fuel to the fire of his critics.

For all the flaws of the first edition, however, its significance in the history of New Testament studies can hardly be overstated. Roland Bainton described the importance of having the Greek New Testament in print for the first time: "The mere fact alone that the New Testament in Greek was available in book form, whatever the text, was of immense significance, because thereby the task of collation was expedited. Manuscripts could not be transported from country to country without grave risks. Printed copies could be sent to the manuscripts and variant readings recorded in the margins. Then the books could be gathered and the evidence assembled. If in the process a book were lost, it was not irreplaceable."[24]

In addition to providing the Greek and Latin texts side by side on opposing columns on the same page, the 1516 edition also contained a set of annotations, printed at the back of the volume, and several items of significant front matter. In subsequent editions the annotations would grow larger than the New Testament text itself, eventually requiring a second volume. The annotations included philological comments, variant readings, and textual analysis, but some of them were also content notes in which Erasmus responded to his growing chorus of critics.[25] Erasmus prudently dedicated the volume to Pope Leo X, whom he had met at Rome in 1509 as Giovanni de Medici. The edition of 1519 also included an approving letter of commendation from the Pope, which Erasmus found a helpful feature in fending off charges of heterodoxy from his conservative Catholic critics. There was also an apology defending his efforts to restore the original text and a brief statement on hermeneutics, which would be greatly expanded in the second edition—and later printed as a separate treatise, the *Ratio Verae Theologiae*. The *Ratio* contained Erasmus's recommendations for a proper theological education and a summary of his hermeneutics.

Erasmus's Greek New Testament also included a preface, which he called *Paraclesis*. This is a Greek word that means summons or exhortation, a word closely related to Jesus's depiction of the Holy Spirit as the Paraclete or Counselor (John 15:26). The *Paraclesis* was a passionate plea for the philosophy of Christ. The life of faith, Erasmus argued, is available to everyone regardless of age, gender, fortune, or position in life. No one is excluded, unless a person begrudgingly keeps himself away. In this vein, Erasmus called for the translation of the Bible into the vernacular languages so that the mysteries of Christ could be accessible to all:

> I would that even the lowliest women read
> the Gospels and the Pauline epistles. And
> I would that they were translated into all
> languages so that they could be read and
> understood not only by Scots and Irish, but
> also by Turks and Saracens . . . Would that,
> as a result, the farmer sings some portion
> of them at the plow, the weaver hums some
> parts of them to the movement of his shuttle,
> the traveler lighten the weariness of the
> journey with stories of this kind![26]

Inherent in Erasmus's oft-quoted plea for vernacular translations of the Bible is the doctrine of the spiritual priesthood of all believers. However, it is worth pondering why Erasmus himself never published a single page of Scripture in the vernacular, not even in his native Dutch. H. J. De Jonge has cogently argued that Erasmus was far more interested in his elegant Latin translation of the New Testament than his printing of the Greek text which lay behind it.[27]

Greek was the language of the learned few and the vernacular languages were just coming of age in the sixteenth century. Latin was still a common bond across the various national and language groups in Europe and Erasmus thought of the Bible primarily as a Latin book. He believed that the philosophy of Christ could provide the basis for a Christendom-wide harmony within the empire, the church, and the multilingual cities and nation-states of Europe. Still, however great his expectations for a Bible freshly dressed in polished Latin, he genuinely welcomed efforts to place the word of God in the hands of the common people. "Do you think," Erasmus asked, "that the Scriptures are fit only for the perfumed?"[28]

Erasmus closed the *Paraclesis* with an exhortation for everyone to love, read, and listen to the Bible from earliest childhood until the very hour of death. "These writings bring you the living image of [Christ's] holy mind and the speaking, healing, dying, rising Christ himself, and thus they render Him so fully present that you would see less if you gazed upon Him with your very eyes."[29]

Erasmus next turned his attention to another project: publishing paraphrases of the New Testament. Starting with Romans in 1517, and concluding with Acts in 1524, he covered every book except Revelation – he was neither the first nor the last to find the last book in the Bible resistant to comprehensible summary. The paraphrase was neither a translation nor a commentary, though Erasmus did call it "a kind of commentary." A translation aims to render faithfully an original text from one language into another, if not word for word, at least with close attention to the base text. The commentary is an exegetical explanation or exposition of a given book or treatise, often divided into discrete units corresponding to verses or pericopes in the text being commented on. In style, the paraphrase is something in between these two genres. As he put it, the purpose of a paraphrase is to "say things differently without saying different things."[30]

In the Paraphrases, Erasmus sought to fulfill what he had promised in the *Paraclesis*. Through his own smooth, eloquent restating/paraphrasing of the New Testament, he would inculcate the "love of divine books through the beauty of language." Like all theologians including "grammarians," as his scholastic critics called him, Erasmus wrote with an agenda, even when he protested that he had no agenda. The Paraphrases reveal a distinctively Erasmian pattern of biblical interpretation. Uppermost in his mind is the moral sense of the text, for ethics rather than doctrine was his main concern.

As a disciple of Origen, Erasmus is drawn toward allegorical interpretations, even when the plain reading of the text does not require such. For example, in his paraphrase of the story of Jesus asleep in the boat in the midst of the storm, Erasmus surmises that there must have been many other boats on the Sea of Galilee at the time, though the body of Jesus was present in only one of them. Just so, he claims, "There is one Catholic Church but there are many churches. Christ is in all of them equally and when all adhere to him as the one head, then the church is one. No ship is wrecked which follows Christ."[31] Erasmus does not tell us the other churches he has in mind. Perhaps the churches of the East? The emerging Protestant communities? The invisible church of pious souls moved by inward piety but distrustful of all ecclesial structures? In any event, Erasmus finds in this gospel story a wider ecclesiology than that allowed by the traditional interpretation of "outside the church there is no salvation."

Through the Paraphrases, Erasmus spread the philosophy of Christ among Europe's pastors and literate laity from Leiden to Lithuania. Erasmus wrote the Paraphrases in Latin but they were soon translated into the vernaculars. The reception of Erasmus' Paraphrases in England was a special case. Katherine Parr, the sixth wife of Henry VIII, and the only one to outlive her husband, was a major figure in turning the Reformation in England in an explicitly Protestant direction.[32] She herself was an author of several devotional works and also extended patronage to such high-profile reformers as Hugh Latimer and Nicholas Ridley. Katherine arranged for the Paraphrases to be translated into English. In 1547, King Edward VI issued a royal injunction requiring that the Paraphrases, along with a copy of the English Bible, be publicly displayed in every single parish in the Church of England. The same requirement was reinstituted at the accession of Elizabeth in 1559.

While some have questioned the real impact of the Paraphrases on the course of the English Reformation, John Craig's study of their reception led him to a different conclusion. According to Craig, the Paraphrases were "widely purchased and used; they helped to make the New Testament in English available and known to clergy and people; and they were the chief means by which Erasmus was claimed for the English reformed church."[33] Nicholas Udall, a Tudor playwright who supervised the English paraphrase project presents Erasmus as a true proto-Protestant, "the chief leader and shower of light and the principal opener of a way unto the evangelical truth now in these last times by God's goodness shining forth into the world."[34]

The Forerunner?

"Erasmus laid the egg that Luther hatched." This old saw was coined in the 1520s by some of Erasmus's detractors within the Franciscan community at Cologne. Soon it was on the lips of everyone. When someone asked Erasmus what he thought about this saying, he admitted to having laid the egg, but he said that Luther's chicks were a different kind of bird.[35]

To move from poultry to bread making, a popular broadsheet called "The Divine Mill" (1521) depicted Erasmus and Luther working side by side to produce the harvest of the gospel.

The Divine Mill

This image was a revamping of an earlier fifteenth-century woodcut, called the Host Mill, which visually portrayed the Catholic doctrine of transubstantiation. In the Reformation version of the mill image, Christ pours into the hopper the four evangelists represented by their traditional symbols. Erasmus supervised the milling process and takes the flour which comes forth in little cakes called faith, hope, love, and the church. Standing next to Erasmus, Luther distributes the bread of life in the form of gospel books to the pope, a bishop, a monk, and a nun, all of whom refuse to receive Luther's offerings, allowing the books to fall to the ground. Above this scene stands the peasant Karsthans, with scythe in hand, threatening to wreak divine vengeance on those who refuse to heed the Reformation message. Here, humanism and reformation are allies in a common cause; Erasmus mills the flour that Luther bakes.[36]

In traditional Reformation historiography, Erasmus often appears at the end of a long line of forerunners, precursors who anticipated the teachings of the sixteenth-century reformers and even prepared the way for their advent. Among these *Reformers before the Reformation,* to use the title of a famous book by Karl Heinrich Ullmann published in the nineteenth century, Erasmus stands with the likes of John Wycliffe, John Hus, Wesel Gansfort, Savonarola, and others. Apart from the fact that this interpretation turns such characters into stage props for the main show, Erasmus hardly fits the pattern because he was a participant observer of the events he helped to precipitate.[37]

For a while it seemed to almost everyone that Erasmus and Luther were rowing on the same team. When the Greek New Testament came out in March 1516, Luther was lecturing on the Epistle to the Romans in Wittenberg. The manuscript of his lectures reveals that from chapter nine forward he was drawing insights from the Greek text and annotations of Erasmus, which he frequently cites. He shows respect for the opinions "of Erasmus and of those who agree with him" even when his own studies lead to different exegetical conclusions.[38] Clearly Luther appreciated the philological prowess of Erasmus, but already he chided the great humanist for failing to grasp the gravity of sin and the true dilemma of the human before God. The knowledge of the biblical languages was important but not sufficient for grasping the true meaning of Scripture. No one is a wise Christian just because he knows Greek and Hebrew, Luther quipped.

Albert Rabil, Jr. has compared Luther's Romans lectures of 1516 with Erasmus's Paraphrases on Romans published in the following year. He sees in their respective approaches to Romans a contrast of theological vision that would lead to their great debate over the bondage and freedom of the will in 1524-1525.

> Erasmus and Luther are very much alike and at the same time very different. For Erasmus, man is basically good, though finite, and the question is how man acts; for Luther, man is a sinner, and the question is the conditions under which he can act. It follows that for Erasmus there is continuity between the old and the new man, as there is between Christ and Moses and between nature and grace. For Luther there is a radical discontinuity: the new man is a man for the first time, Christ abrogates the Mosaic covenant, and grace annuls rather than perfects nature. Further, for Erasmus, God is a kind Father and Christ the perfect exemplification and pattern of the virtues derived from a kind father. For Luther, God is a Father who shows his kindness only through his wrath but once we have passed through the fire of God's wrath we find Christ who is indeed the perfect exemplification of the kindness of God. For Erasmus, faith in Christ renders us righteous or potentially so, given this faith, the choice of action is up to us. For Luther, faith in Christ *is* our righteousness and

there is nothing we can do either before or after that righteousness to make it manifest. Nonetheless, we will do so, for a man *does* as he *is*. The sign of his doing will be suffering in the world, for the man of grace is so unlike nature that he can only relate to it by opposition.[39]

However profound their differences though, Erasmus was indeed the miller who provided the flour for Luther's evangelical bakery. In the first of his Ninety-five Theses, Luther declared, "When our Lord and Master Jesus Christ said, 'Repent,' He willed the entire life of believers to be one of repentance."[40] The true understanding of *poenitentia* had been at the center of Luther's tortured conscience in the monastery. He knew that without true *poenitentia* there could be no reconciliation with God, and yet his own struggles in the confessional left him mired in desperation, for he realized that he could never fulfill adequately the requirements of the sacrament of penance. It was Johan von Staupitz, his confessor and spiritual father, who helped him to overcome his servile fear about his lack of a right standing before God by pointing him to the cross and "the wounds of the sweetest Savior."[41]

Luther's evangelical breakthrough was followed by an exegetical one when he realized that the traditional Vulgate rendering of Matthew 3:2 as *poenitentium agite,* "do penance," was a mistranslation of the Greek. Luther learned from Erasmus that the Greek word *metanoia* was derived from *meta* and *nous,* meaning "afterwards" and "mind," "so that *poenitentia* or *metanoia* means a coming to one's senses . . . the emphasis on works of penance had come from the misleading [Vulgate] translation, which indicates an action rather than a change of heart and in no way corresponds to Greek *metanoia.*"[42]

In his note on Matthew 3:2, Erasmus criticized those theologians who connected this text with the works of satisfaction in the sacrament of penance. "Our people think that *poenitentium agite* means to wash away one's sins with some prescribed penalty ... yet *metanoia* is derived from *metanoein*, that is, to come to one's senses afterwards when someone who sinned, finally after the fact, recognizes his error."[43]

What Jesus and John the Baptist preached in the Gospel of Matthew was not penance but penitence, that is, repentance. And repentance was the habit of a lifetime, not a series of one-off responses or prescribed acts intended to assuage a guilty conscience. Erasmus never drew the radical conclusions Luther came to concerning the sacrament of penance. In his 1522 edition of the New Testament, under pressure from his Catholic critics, Erasmus reverted to the traditional Latin translation of *metanoeite, poenitentiam agite.* But by then the damage had been done.

As lines began to be drawn in the sand, Erasmus chose to be, as he put it, "a spectator rather than an actor."[44] At the behest of Melanchthon, Luther wrote a fawning letter in March 1518, stating, "Who is there in whose heart Erasmus does not occupy a central place, to whom Erasmus is not the teacher who holds him enthralled ... and so, dear Erasmus, accept this younger brother of yours in Christ." Seeing Luther's flattery for what it was, Erasmus responded with a polite but curt thank you note.[45] Luther's true sentiment came out in a letter he wrote to his friend Johann Lang on March 1, 1517, "I am reading our Erasmus but daily I dislike him more and more ... Human things weigh more with him than the divine."[46]

For his part, Erasmus called for fair treatment for Luther in the wake of his excommunication and hearing before the Diet of Worms in 1521. If Luther were to be crushed, he reasoned, then the bloodhounds would soon be on his own tracks and everything for which he had given his life, the whole project of *bonae litterae*, could go up in flames. Privately, Erasmus spoke either favorably or disapprovingly about Luther, depending on the person to whom he wrote. The pressure mounted for him to cease playing Mr. Facing-Both-Ways and to attack Luther in print. The pressures came from the emperor, Charles V, from Duke George of Saxony, from Henry VIII in England, and from Pope Adrian VI, Erasmus's fellow Dutchman, and the last non-Italian pope until John Paul II. The result was Erasmus's blast on free will, and Luther's counter-blast on the will's thralldom. The rest is history.

If Erasmus thought his diatribe against Luther would quell his critics within the old church, he was mistaken. In the summer of 1526, he reported that he had just received from the presses in Paris "five volumes full of rabid accusations against me."[47] Erasmus never became a gung-ho partisan on either side and remained under suspicion in both camps. He hated the verbal violence, which, he rightly saw, was a likely prelude to religious war. He would not become a *carnifex*, a cannibal, he said. But neither would he volunteer for the martyr's pyre. Nothing pleased Erasmus more than a cozy dinner by a warm fire with good conversation and a flask of well-aged wine from Crete (his favorite). "Let others court martyrdom," he remarked. "I don't consider myself worthy of this distinction."[48]

As late as 1518, Erasmus said that he thought he could see a golden age dawning in the near future.[49] The events into which he was invariably if reluctantly drawn

Thinking Christianly: *Christian Higher Education and a Vigorous Life of the Mind* dampened his optimism. A few years later, he was referring to his time as "the worst century since Jesus Christ."[50] From Basel, he wrote to his friend Willibald Pirckheimer, a fellow humanist and patron of letters, "Peace is perishing, and love and faith and learning and morality and civilized behavior. What is left?"[51]

But the Erasmian moment outlasted Erasmus. Both Luther and Tyndale had copies of his 1519 Greek New Testament at hand as they labored to "verdeutschen" and "english" God's Word for the farmers, ploughboys, pimps, and prostitutes of Germany and England. The debate between Erasmus and Luther on the bondage of the will did not result in the divorce of humanism and the Reformation. The torch had been passed to a new generation of reformers for whom the *studia humanitatis* and *theologia crucis* were both central in the renewal of the church.

References:

[1] István Bejczy, *Erasmus and the Middle Ages: The Historical Consciousness of a Christian Humanist* (Leiden: Brill, 2001), 113. CWE 12:179; EE 6:328 (no.1700).

[2] *The Epistles of Erasmus*, ed. F. N. Nichols (London, 1901) 2:163, 327.

[3] WATR 1. no. 131; LW 54:19, "Erasmus is an eel. Nobody can grasp him except Christ alone. He is a double-dealing man."

[4] *Advocates of Reform from Wycliffe to Erasmus*, ed. Matthew Spinka (Philadelphia: Westminster, 1953), 378.

[5] See István Bejczy, *Erasmus and the Middle Ages*, 96-101.

[6] CWE 8:227; EE 4:508 (no. 1211).

[7] EE 1:190-93 (no. 64); CWE 1:136-37.

[8] John C. Olin, *Six Essays on Erasmus* (New York: Fordham University Press, 1979), 33.

[9] See Eileen Bloch, "Erasmus and the Froben Press: The Making of an Editor," *The Library Quarterly* 35 (1965), 109-20.

[10] CWE 3:260-61; EE 2:216 (no. 396). See the discussion in Eugene F. Rice, Jr., *St. Jerome in the Renaissance* (Baltimore: Johns Hopkins University Press, 1985), 116-36.

[11] WA 7, 142, 30. Quoted, Manfred Schulze, "Martin Luther and the Church Fathers," in *The Reception of the Church Fathers in the West*, ed. Irena Backus (Leiden: Brill, 1997) 2:621. For a similar concession by Calvin, see his *Institutes* 3.11.15.

[12] In his *Lectures on Genesis*, in the context of discussing the foreshadowing of the Trinity in the appearance of the three visitors to Abraham in Genesis 18, Luther makes this parenthetical comment about the fathers and the doctrine of justification by faith: "After I know that we are justified by faith alone – for, like a dialectical argument, this has been abundantly proved and set forth in Holy Scripture – it pleases me very much that Augustine, Hilary, Cyril, and Ambrose say the same thing, even though they do not stress the foundations so much and at times express themselves less properly. I do not charge that this is an error on their part. It is enough for me that they say the same thing, even though they say it less properly; and I am strengthened by their testimony, in spite of the fact that it is more rhetorical than dialectical." LW 3, 194-95.

[13] On sixteenth-century patristic anthologies, see the following studies by Anthony N. S. Lane: "Early Printed Patristic Anthologies to 1566: A Progress Report," *Studia Patristica* 18 (1990), 365-70; "Justification in Sixteenth-Century Patristics," in *Auctoritas Patrum* (Mainz: Phillipp von Zabern, 1993), 69-93; *John Calvin: Student of the Church Fathers* (Grand Rapids: Baker Books, 1999).

[14] *Works of John Jewel* 4:1173-74.

---

[15] Eugene Rice, *Jerome in the Renaissance*, 3.

[16] John Colet, *An Exposition of St. Paul's First Epistle to the Corinthians*, ed. J. H. Lupton, 110-11, 238-39. See Schwarz, *Principles and Problems of Biblical Translation*, 113.

[17] The idea of "spoiling the Egyptians" was bequeathed to Augustine by Origen (MG 11.88-89). Augustine refers to the use by the children of Israel of the spoils of Egypt in adorning the Lord's Temple in *De Doctrina Christiana* 2.40.61.

[18] See Konrad Pelikan, *Reformation of the Bible/Bible of the Reformation*, 3.

[19] On Erasmus's knowledge of Hebrew, see Erika Rummel, "The Textual and Hermeneutic Work of Desiderius Erasmus of Rotterdam," in *Hebrew Bible/Old Testament,* ed. Magne Sæbø (Göttingen, Germany: Vandenoeck & Ruprecht, 2008) 219-21. For "nibbled" see LB 5, 78C-79A.

[20] See Michael J. Heath's remark about Erasmus's commentary on Psalm 2. "Erasmus's enforced preference for rhetorical effect over textual accuracy, which shocked some contemporary critics, even led him to conclude, with a touch of bravado, that the Greek and Latin versions of the Psalms provided all the information and, especially, all the inspiration required by the exegete. It also made him indifferent to Hebrew itself; considering the different meanings of the word *bar* (a son? purity? wheat?) in Syriac and Hebrew, he cuts the discussion short with a dismissive pun: 'There is no need to cudgel our brains with complexities of these barbaric languages.' This is his only contribution to Jerome's erudite discussion of Psalm 2:12." "Erasmus and the Psalms," in Richard Griffiths, ed., *The Bible and the Renaissance: Essays on Biblical Commentary and Translation in the Fifteenth and Sixteenth Centuries* (Aldershot: Ashgate, 2001), 38-39.

[21] Ibid, 220. On the question of whether or to what extent Erasmus exhibited the traits of anti-Semitism, see Shimon Markish, *Erasmus and the Jews* (Chicago: University of Chicago Press, 1986), and especially the rejoinder by Arthur A. Cohen published in the same volume. Heiko A. Oberman places the views of Erasmus in the wider context of Reformation attitudes toward the Jews. See his *The Roots of Anti-Semitism* (Philadelphia: Fortress Press, 1981). See also Erika Rummel, "Humanists, Jews, and Judaism" in Dean Phillip Bell and

Stephen G. Burnett, *Jews, Judaism, and the Reformation in Sixteenth-Century Germany* (Leiden: Brill, 2006), 3-32. Roland Bainton goes too far when he declares, "Erasmus would not have found it difficult to be a Marcionite." Bainton, *Erasmus*, 143. His 1533 treatise, *De sarcienda ecclesiae concordia*, "On Restoring the Unity of the Church," Erasmus excoriates the "manichaeans" for their Marcionite-like belief that the entire Old Testament should be rejected as "something handed down not by God but by the Prince of Darkness." See Raymond Himelick, trans., *Erasmus and the Seamless Coat of Jesus* (Lafayette, Indiana: Purdue University Press, 1971), 13.

[22] See Johann Huizinga, *Erasmus and the Age of Reformation* (New York: Harper and Row, 1924), 57.

[23] EE 3:117 (no.694); CWE 5:167.

[24] Roland Bainton, *Erasmus*, 134.

[25] Erika Rummel has catalogued some of these controversies and described Erasmus's response in her *Erasmus' Annotations on the New Testament from Philologist to Theologian* (Toronto: University of Toronto Press, 1986). See also Jerry H. Bentley, *Humanists and Holy Writ: New Testament Scholarship in the Renaissance* (Princeton: Princeton University Press, 1983). 112-93.

[26] John C. Olin, ed., *Christian Humanism and the Reformation* (Fordham: Fordham University Press, 1987), 101.

[27] H. J. De Jonge, "*Novum Testamentum a Nobis Versum*: The Essence of Erasmus' Edition of the New Testament," *Journal of Theological Studies* 35 (1984), 394-413.

[28] Roland Bainton, 141.

[29] Olin, *Humanism and the Reformation*, 108.

[30] CWE 5:196; EE 3:138 (no. 710).

[31] LB 7, 192E. Quoted, Roland H. Bainton, "The Paraphrases of Erasmus," *ARG* 57 (1966), 72

[32] On Parr, Janel Mueller, "Katherine Parr," in OER 3:221-22.

---

[33] Ibid, 335.

[34] Quoted in John Craig, "Forming a Protestant Consciousness? Erasmus' *Paraphases* in English Parishes, 1547-1666," in *Holy Scripture Speaks: The Production and Reception of Erasmus' Paraphrases on the New Testament*, eds. Hilmar M. Pabel and Mark Vessey (Toronto: University of Toronto Press, 2002), 320.

[35] CWE 10:464; EE 5:609 (no. 1528). *"Ego posui ouum gallinaceum, Luthesus exclusit pullum longe dissimillimum."*

[36] On "The Divine Mill," see Andrew Pettegree, *Reformation in the Culture of Persuasion* (Cambridge: Cambridge University Press, 2005), 111-17.

[37] Heiko Oberman includes a chapter on Erasmus in his *Forerunners of the Reformation* (Philadelphia: Fortress Press, 1966). Oberman defends the concept of the Forerunner of the Reformation as "a valid and indispensible tool for historical interpretation," but qualifies the concept in three important ways: (1) that forerunners have explanatory but not causative connections to the Reformation; (2) that the concept of forerunner be broadened beyond Luther and the doctrine of justification by faith to include figures such as Zwingli, Bucer, and later reformers; (3) that the reform programs of pre-reformation forerunners have multiple outcomes in both the Protestant and the Catholic Reformation.

[38] *Luther: Lectures on Romans*, ed. Wilhelm Pauck (Philadelphia: Westminster Press, 1961), 419.

[39] Albert Rabil, Jr., *Erasmus and the New Testament: The Mind of a Christian Humanist* (San Antonio: Trinity University Press, 1972), 178-79.

[40] LW 31, 83.

[41] LW 48, 66.

[42] WA 1/1 525:24-27. Quoted in Rummel, *Erasmus's Annotations*, 153.

[43] Ibid, 152.

[44] CWE 8:78; EE 4:371 (no. 1155). *"Ego huius fabulae spectator esse malim quam histrio."* This letter was addressed to Reuchlin in 1520.

⁴⁵ EE 3:516-19, 605-7 (nos. 933 and 980); CWE 6:281-83, 391-93.

⁴⁶ WABr 1, 90, 15; LW 48, 40.

⁴⁷ CWE 12:326; EE 6:399 (no.1743). One of these volumes was by Noel Beda, opponent of the new trilingual course of studies at Paris and Erasmus's *bête noir.*

⁴⁸ CWE 8:120-1; EE 4:410 (no.1167).

⁴⁹ CWE 27:48.

⁵⁰ CWE 8:315; EE 4:594-95 (no. 1239); "Non arbitror a Christo nato seculum fuisse hoc maliciosius."

⁵¹ CWE 13:401; EE 7:216-17 (no. 1893); "Perit concordia, charitas, fides, disciplinae, mores, ciuilitas. Quid superest?"

Editor's Note:

Fisher Humphreys joined Samford University's Beeson Divinity School faculty in 1990 as a professor of theology and served until he retired in 2008. An award-winning professor, Humphreys is the author of more than ten books. He shares that his first contact with Tom was ". . .when he gave a series of lectures at the seminary where I was teaching. I was immensely impressed by the lectures and thought that I'd like to get to know him personally." Humphreys confides that he finally got to meet Tom when he joined the Samford faculty, and they developed a friendship as they discovered mutual interests, and says, "I admired him immensely and treasured our friendship."

▲ Tom with his family at son Chris's wedding, February 2008. L-R Jennifer, Tom, Marla, Chris, and Rachel.

▲ Known as an eloquent speaker, here is Tom gesturing in a familiar speaking pose.

▲ Marla and Tom at their retirement dinner, April 2006.

▲ Thousands of Wingate and Samford diplomas bear Tom's signature, and he took great effort to sign each personally.

▶ Personally signing diplomas with a Mont Blanc pen in deep blue ink was a Tom Corts trademark.

▲ *A pensive Tom Corts on the Samford campus in late fall of 1983, at age 42.*

▲ *Tom and Marla during their first semester on the Samford campus in 1983.*

▲ *Tom with his siblings on the occasion of a convocation at Beeson Divinity School in 2001 organized by Dean Timothy George, entitled: "Six Remarkable Leaders." L-R Tom, David, John, Naomi, Mark, and Paul.*

▼ *Tom in 2006 seated on a bench beside the statue of Ralph Beeson – a piece of art Tom meticulously directed to honor this generous benefactor.*

▼ *Tom, about 1969, while serving as Special Assistant to the President under President Robert L. Mills at Georgetown College.*

▲ This photo shows Tom and Marla at the presentation of the Marla Haas Corts Missionary Biography Collection which Tom had personally purchased over the years and gave to Samford in honor of his wife and in appreciation for her service to Samford.

◄ Tom with President Gerald Ford at the dedication of the Lucille Stewart Beeson Law Library in 1996.

◄ L-R: Former Samford President Leslie Wright, Trustee Gerow Hodges, and Tom at the unveiling of the portrait of Frank Park Samford (for whom the University is named) in the background.

▲ Tom brought football back to Samford and is shown here with Coach Terry Bowden and members of the football team.

▲ Tom receiving a presentation from the Athletic Department celebrating 20 years of Samford football, 1984-2004.

▲ Tom along with members of the administrative staff performing in Samford's Step Sing. Tom is second from left.

▲ Tom with U. S. Senator Jeff Sessions (Alabama) speaking at commencement for Samford's Cumberland School of Law in 2001.

▲ Tom with members of his family attending his inauguration in 1983. L-R: (first row) Rachel, Marla, Charles, Tom, Chris, Hazel, Ruth Haas, Jennifer; (second row) Amy, Shirley, Naomi White, Debi White; (third row) Phillip, George White, Mark, and Paul.

▼ Tom and Marla with President George W. Bush and Laura at the White House Christmas reception in 2007.

◀ Tom (with the Samford bulldog mascot) standing beside Chick-fil-A founder Truett Cathy who is serving a bite of chicken to his Chick-fil-A mascot at the Chick-fil-A kiosk on the Samford campus.

◀ Tom in his new office at Samford in 1983.

▼ L-R: Emmett Johnson (CEO, Birmingham Baptist Health System), Tom and Ida V. Moffett, retired Dean of the Ida V. Moffett School of Nursing at a presentation of her just-released biography, Courage to Care, in 1988.

▲ Tom with his brother Paul at Tom's inauguration in 1983.

◀ A very happy Tom at his retirement dinner, April 2006.

▲ Tom with British Prime Minister John Major who spoke at Samford in 1997.

▲ Tom with his mentor Robert L. Mills who served as president of Georgetown College from 1959-1978, at Tom's inauguration in 1983.

▲ At Tom's inauguration in 1983, son Chris holds the Bible during Tom's investiture as Samford President; wife Marla and daughters Jennifer and Rachel look on.

▲ Tom at his inauguration with his parents Charles Harold Corts and Hazel Louise Vernon Corts.

▼ Former Samford President Leslie Wright giving new president Tom Corts a campus tour in 1983.

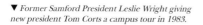

▲ Tom seated on stage in 2006 near the end of his Samford tenure.

▲ Tom with British Prime Minister Margaret
Thatcher who was speaking at Samford in 1992.

▲ Tom packing up his office and preparing to leave
Samford in 2006.

▲ Tom with U. S. Attorney General Janet Reno
who spoke at the Cordell Hull Speakers Forum in
Samford's Cumberland School of Law.

◄ Tom with
his family on
the occasion
of Chris and
Lesley's
wedding,
February 2008.

► Tom and Marla with noted musician Dave Brubeck who
performed at a special inaugural event in 1983.

When the last check is written,
  the lone remaining bill is paid,
  ev'ry IOU is cancelled,
  payment on accounts is stayed;
When the parting farewell is uttered,
  the ending stanza sung,
  benediction's ended,
  tolling bells have rung;
I still will debtor be
  throughout eternity;
Not all the gold in banks
  fulfills my debt of thanks.
          - Thomas Corts

CHAPTER 7

A CHRISTIAN UNIVERSITY:
EXPLORING ONE OF ITS ASPIRATIONS

By Fisher Humphreys

A year and a half after President Thomas E. Corts died so unexpectedly, two memories of him keep returning to me. The first concerns a committee that he appointed in the 1990s to prepare a full and balanced mission statement for Samford University. About a dozen persons served on the committee, including Corts. He was not the chair. At the committee meetings, everyone contributed to the document, arguing energetically for or against each other's proposals. Some of Corts's proposals made it into the document and others did not. Because he did not attempt to dominate the meetings, every committee member was at liberty to contribute his or her best ideas. The outcome was a document of which, I believe, all of us were proud.

The second memory, from a few years later, concerns a seminar led by William E. Hull following his retirement from the office of provost of Samford University. The theme of the seminar was "a Christian university." The members of the seminar were faculty and staff of the university who chose to participate. Among those was Corts. Once again, he made no effort to dominate the group's meetings. On one occasion an especially feisty faculty member insisted at some length that Samford's mission statement was inferior and sub-Christian. He said, among other things, that the mission statement did not even mention Jesus. When it was pointed out to him that the mission statement did in fact speak of Jesus, he replied, "Well, it doesn't mention Him until near the end." Throughout this dialogue Dr. Corts said nothing, simply listening.

As I observed Dr. Corts in those settings, I developed a conviction that one of the most urgent tasks in his life was to make Samford as Christian a university as possible. I would not be in the least surprised to learn that Dr. Corts began every day of his life by asking himself, "What can I do today to help Samford be a more Christian university?"

In this essay, I want to offer a few ideas about a Christian university. I think these ideas are basic, so basic that they are often overlooked.

The Phrase *A Christian University*

On three occasions the word Christian is used in the Bible, always as a noun and never as an adjective. The followers of Jesus in Antioch were the first persons to be called Christians (Acts 11:26). King Herod Agrippa II sensed that the apostle Paul was trying to persuade him to become a Christian (Acts 26:28). Peter assured his readers that it was not disgraceful to suffer as a Christian (1 Peter 4:16). The fact that none of these uses is adjectival means that, in the book that serves as the written authority for faith and life for the followers of Jesus, there is no normative usage of *Christian* as an adjective.

Universities as we know them today are the result of a movement that began in the Middle Ages. Many of the early European universities originated in monasteries. Priests and monks became adept at teaching theology and Bible and canon law and so on, and young men (it was all males in the medieval period) came to hear them lecture and to engage in debate about the subjects. Other subjects were also taught, including law and medicine. Later the curriculum expanded to include the liberal arts. The universities acquired extensive libraries and began to award degrees. There is a direct historical line between universities such as Oxford and Paris and universities such as Samford.

The Bible does not mention universities, of course, since universities in the sense described above did not exist during the biblical era. Since the Bible neither contains an adjectival use of the word Christian nor mentions universities, it offers no help to those who want an authorized definition of the phrase Christian university. This means that Christians have a great deal of latitude in how they use the phrase.

It is quite reasonable, therefore, for someone to say, "By Christian university I mean a university which was founded by a church, which is funded by that church, which has a clergy person as president, which has only persons committed to Christ on its governing board, which employs only Christians as faculty, which admits only Christians as students, and which requires that all its members live in conformity with New Testament moral teachings." At the opposite extreme, it is equally reasonable for someone to say, "By Christian university I mean a university with an institutional commitment to certain ideals of the Christian religion, such as truthfulness." In the absence of an authorized definition of Christian university, it is a waste of energy to debate which of these usages is more appropriate.

Of course, there are limits to the ways Christian university may be used. For example, it would be nonsense to describe an educational institution devoted to the dissemination of atheism as a Christian university, just as it would be nonsense to describe a kindergarten as a Christian university. But within fairly broad limits, there are many variations on how the phrase Christian university may reasonably be used. It is wise, therefore, to say, "I realize that it is appropriate that others use the phrase Christian university in other ways. What I can do is to tell you how I am going to use it." I am going to use it to refer to a university that aspires to live out certain ideals that Christians hold dear.

Aspirations of a Christian University

Consider two questions: "Am I a Christian?" and "Am I Christian?" Many followers of Christ would answer the first question in the affirmative, and they would do so energetically and confidently. They are not Muslims, nor are they atheists. They are Christians. This answer is not a boast. It is simply a meaningful and accurate description. But most followers of Christ probably would answer the second question in a different way. They would say, "I want to be Christian. I am trying to be Christian. I hope to be more Christian in the future." This is not false modesty. It is also a meaningful and accurate description.

Why do the two questions receive such different answers? I think it is because the adjective Christian, unlike the noun, connotes ideals to which those who are attempting to follow Jesus aspire. They do not claim to live out these ideals fully. They do claim that they aspire to do so and are attempting to do so.

This leads to several questions. To what ideals do Christians aspire? What Christian beliefs have generated these ideals? Where are these ideals operative in the life of a university? Who bears the responsibility to maintain these ideals in a university? How are these ideals related to the ideals of a university? A comprehensive answer to these questions could fill a large book. What I will try to do here is to address just one ideal in the hope that it could serve as an example of how other ideals might be addressed. Like most Christian ideals, that ideal arises out of an identifiable Christian belief.

Students and the Image of God

Oxford University comprises about forty colleges, one of which is All Souls. All Souls is famous for several things, including the high quality of food and drink served in its hall and the fact that it has no undergraduate students. Its faculty, who are called *fellows*, may and sometimes do teach undergraduate students of the university, but that is optional. The fellows' sole responsibility is to carry on with the research and writing that led to their being invited to become fellows. The college has no students of its own. This may make All Souls unique among the world's colleges. For everyone else, students are indispensable.

Christians believe that all human beings, including university students, have been created in the image of God. This understanding of human beings appears first in the creation story (Genesis 1:27), and it reappears about a dozen times elsewhere in the Bible. Because the Bible nowhere defines the image of God, it is understandable that Christians have made a variety of proposals about it. Among other things, the image has been understood to be humans' awareness of right and wrong, their reason, their creativity, their dominion over the rest of creation, and their capacity for interpersonal relationships of trust and love. Christians agree that the image is a similarity between God and human beings, a similarity that is unique to human beings in that it was given to human beings in creation rather than acquired by human activity.

This similarity to God is the source of the dignity and value of human beings. A classic passage is Psalms 8:5: "You have made them a little lower than God, and crowned them with glory and honor." These words were written of human beings following their fall into sin and therefore apply to all human beings today and not just the first human beings.

So the students in a modern university have been made a little lower than God. They bear the image of God, and they are crowned by God with glory and honor. Clearly creatures such as these should be treated with respect. One aspiration of a Christian university is to respect its students.

Respecting Students

What does it mean for a university to respect its students? It means that the university takes an interest in them and their lives. Administrators and faculty members who care, not just about whether or not students are learning and developing skills but also about their lives apart from learning, are respecting their students. It also means that the university will appreciate its students.

Administrators and faculty members are respecting their students when they appreciate them. They can appreciate them as persons made in God's image before they know anything about their work, and they can come to appreciate them as students when their work is good work. A great deal of human striving is a quest to find respect, caring, and appreciation. What must it mean to a student, who has deep needs for respect and caring and appreciation, to find these things in the faculty and administrators of a university?

Various things can prevent faculty and staff from giving students the respect, care, and appreciation they need. One is that the faculty and staff have not experienced these things in their own lives. To the extent that they are still scrambling to obtain them for themselves, they will find it difficult to give them to students. Another thing that prevents faculty and staff from giving these things to students is that some students act in ways that are at variance with their being bearers of God's image. They do not study, they behave as if they know more than their teachers do, they plagiarize, they are chronically late with work, or they are contemptuous of learning. How can faculty and staff care for students whose lives are banal? How can they appreciate students whose work is slack, derivative, and trite?

One thing that helps is to remember that much of these students' behavior arises from fear. It is intimidating to be an authentic student. Students naturally think: My mind is so small. The subject is so large. How can I ever grasp even a part of what they have known? When faculty and staff recognize that students' irresponsibility is a product of their fears, they can respond to it appropriately without losing the conviction that the students are bearers of God's image.

My wife Caroline and I have two adult children. When they were young I noticed something anomalous. We had to begin treating our children as responsible before they actually were responsible. By treating them as responsible, we helped them to become responsible and to behave responsibly. So it is, I think, with university students. As a university treats its students as persons worthy of respect, care, and appreciation, the university empowers them to behave as such. In some cases that has to be done before their behavior warrants it. It has to be done, in other words, in hope, with the expectation that treating them as responsible persons will help them to become responsible.

The opposite of respecting and appreciating students is to look upon them with contempt. To treat people with contempt is both a factual error and moral failure. It jeopardizes the work of a university, since only the most superficial learning can take place when students sense that they are held in contempt by the university. Holding people in contempt is something that sometimes is done inadvertently, but it can be done because one has adopted attitudes that justify it. One of the most spiritually helpful questions Christians can ask themselves is this: Upon what person, or group of persons, do I feel entitled to look with contempt?

Professors are tempted to look with contempt upon several kinds of students – students who do poor work, students who are socially awkward or otherwise unattractive, and students who are politically, culturally, or religiously reactionary. Some professors reserve their respect only for graduate students. Many years ago a math instructor in an Ivy League university said to me, "Unfortunately, I have to teach an introductory course for the engineers." By becoming clear about what groups professors feel entitled to look upon with contempt, they learn something important about themselves, and they detect a moral and spiritual project upon which to work. To the extent that they address it successfully, they become not only better Christians but also better teachers and administrators in the university.

Retrieving an Old Virtue

There is, in the Christian tradition, a word for treating people with respect. It is an old-fashioned word, difficult to rehabilitate in our world. But retrieving it can greatly assist professors and administrators in taking seriously their commitment to be a Christian university.
That word is humility. Humility is not contempt for oneself, as is widely assumed. Rather, it is respect for others as well as for oneself. It is recognition that the lives of others are just as important as one's own life. Humility is also respect for God, letting God be God.

In her book *To Pray and to Love*, author Roberta Bondi says that the desert mothers and fathers of the early church understood humility as "the master virtue that includes all the others." She tells the story of Abba Macarius, a monk who, upon returning from a swamp to his cell, was attacked by the devil. The devil struck at him several times with a scythe but could not hurt him. The Abba was puzzled and asked the devil why he could not hurt him. The devil replied, "Your humility. Because of that I can do nothing against you."[1]

Outside of the church, few people seem to appreciate

the Christian commitment to humility. This is surprising, since humility has much to be said for it. For one thing, it is an appropriate response to reality. Other people do matter, and God alone is God. Furthermore, humility is a quality that is essential for a wise life. It is foolish to give one's ultimate allegiance to idols and not to God. It is foolish not to recognize the value of the lives of others.

Humility is also indispensable to authentic community. A superficial community can evolve simply because people are in proximity to others. That is what is found in classrooms where students are not meaningfully engaged in the learning process. A deeper level of community develops when its members share in common tasks to which they are all committed. That is what is found in classrooms where students study the subject matter with a view to making good grades and getting well-paying jobs.

But community in the fullest sense of the word emerges only when members respect one another, when they care about one another's well-being, and when they appreciate the importance of one another's lives. That is what is found in classrooms where a professor respects students in such a way that they are freed from their fears and empowered, not simply to become accumulators of information and skills, but to grow as persons.

Humility empowers human beings to overcome intrinsic self-centeredness. We arrive in this world *incurvatus a se*, curved in upon ourselves. Perhaps that is necessary for our survival, but it is inimical to a meaningful human life. Human beings begin to escape from narcissism when they grasp the fact that they are not God, that only God is God, and that other people bear God's image, just as they do. Humility provides freedom from endless, humorless efforts to justify one's existence. Humble people realize that justification for their existence was given to them when God created them.

Finally, humility can deliver us from contributing to the barrage of petty criticism that characterizes the life of academic communities. Just as it is natural for individuals to be self-centered, so it is natural for members of communities to be cliquish and judgmental. Communities such as universities depend upon news about their members to bind them together, but too often they report news in ways that are untrue, unkind, and unhealthy. Humility, respect for all of the members of the community, provides liberation from that destructive behavior.

How do the faculty and staff in a university express respect for students? Here are some examples. They express respect by learning students' names, by beginning and ending their classes on time, by preparing syllabi and study guides carefully, by listening attentively to students both inside and outside of classrooms, by writing thoughtful and sincere comments on students' papers, by testing that is fair, by giving grades that accurately represent the students' work, and by continuing to challenge as well as affirm students. There is, I think, an ad hoc quality about expressions of respect for students. We don't always know in advance what we will be called upon to do. Guided not only by the expectations of the academy but also by what the Christian faith teaches about the value of persons, Christian faculty and administrators will find ways to express their respect and appreciation for students.

Conclusion

My argument has been that, since there is no authorized biblical definition of the phrase Christian university, Christians have latitude in how they employ the phrase. I use it to refer to a university that aspires to embody ideals that Christians cherish. One of those ideals, respect for all human beings, arises from the Christian belief that all human beings possess a glory and honor given to them by their Creator. The biblical virtue that names this respect is humility. A university honors this commitment by respecting its students. The faculty and staff of a university respect students by taking an interest in them and by appreciating them and their work. They express this respect in many ways, including challenging students to do their best work. Respect for students is one of many ideals that Christians embrace, and it can serve as an example of the kinds of things to which a Christian university aspires.

When Tom Corts asked himself what he could do to help Samford University to become a more fully Christian university, I think he was asking, among other things, how Samford could more fully express respect for its students. By his personal example, by his wise decisions, by his maintenance of the highest standards for life and work, by his noble and gentlemanly conduct, by his friendship, by his determination to behave with integrity despite opposition, distraction, and fatigue, Corts helped Samford to become a more and more fully Christian university. And, to use a phrase that he liked, the world is better for it.

References:

[1]   Roberta C. Bondi, *To Pray and to Love* (Minneapolis: Fortress Press: 1991), 101.

Editor's Note:

One of the most significant issues being discussed in Christian higher education is the "controversy" about how the Bible and orthodox Christian faith comports with science and especially evolution. I recall my brother's early fascination with the great orator William Jennings Bryan and some interesting discussions about Bryan and Clarence Darrow and their rhetorical styles and arguments. As a Christian university president, this religion vs. science topic and the tension that surrounds it would necessarily be part of Tom's work throughout his career. Because in many ways what one thoughtfully believes about creation influences much of the rest of our "thinking Christianly," this essay seemed especially appropriate for this volume. First preached as a sermon, Bill Hull has expanded his sermon to this masterful essay and it shows a part of Bill's extraordinary scholarship and intellect that I know my brother deeply admired, respected, and appreciated.

CHAPTER 8

CHRISTIANITY AND THE EVOLUTION CONTROVERSY

By William E. Hull

Edward Osborne Wilson may well be Alabama's most distinguished living scientist. A biology teacher at Harvard University since 1956, he quickly ascended to the highest ranks of that prestigious faculty where he continues to serve as University Research Professor. The author of more than twenty books and the recipient of more than thirty honorary degrees, Wilson has received almost every scholarly award, recognition, and membership that the academy can bestow. A world-famous entomologist, the acknowledged father of biodiversity, a leading conservationist and environmental activist, he overcame the partial loss of both sight and hearing in his youth to become what *TIME* magazine hailed as one of the twenty-five most influential people in America.

This native son returned home a few days ago and our time spent together reminded me of the many things we share in common. Both of us were born on the south side of Birmingham only a few months apart. Both of us were raised as Southern Baptists by families with deep roots in that denomination. We both attended the University of Alabama at the same time, where we both majored in biology. But then our paths diverged significantly, though we both went on to pursue an academic career. For Wilson, science provided the impetus to abandon his childhood faith, whereas for me, it offered a challenge to mature my very similar childhood faith. Now, a half-century later, we find ourselves at opposite ends of the theological spectrum in our understanding of both natural and supernatural reality.[1]

The two of us would agree that these differences frame one of the most pivotal debates of our time, that between science and religion over the issue of Darwinian evolution. On every hand, media reports on the culture wars have us girding for a fight to the finish between scientism and creationism. Just as the Scopes Trial of 1925 publicly embarrassed evangelical Protestantism for decades, so we are in danger of exposing the Christian faith to unnecessary ridicule unless we learn how to contribute with intelligence and insight to what has become an increasingly acrimonious discussion.[2] Since Wilson is an attractive, articulate, and aggressive advocate of the secular alternative, let us choose him as our dialogue partner in shaping a strategy for dealing with this bitterly contested agenda.

A Naturalist's View of Origins

We begin with a summary of Wilson's views on science and religion. To him, all reality is ultimately physical, with living matter in the domain of biology subject to the laws of chemistry and physics. This means that human nature is the result of material processes, even in the formation of our religious sentiments and moral instincts. In other words, we are "self-assembled" rather than God-assembled.[3] The more science discovers how genetics really work, the less we need theological explanations of our origins rooted in ancient Scripture and church doctrine. Therefore, science and religion should not be viewed as coexisting in separate spheres, the former to explain the physical and the latter to explain the spiritual. Rather, modern science is now ready to replace religion as the unified source of all knowledge. Such views are often referred to as scientific naturalism or secular humanism.

But if God is not the ultimate cause of the human condition, then how did we become what we are today? The answer is self-evident to Wilson: by genetic evolution. That is why he has become such a vigorous defender of Darwinism, which teaches that we evolved by an autonomous process of development determined, not by divine purpose, but by random mutations resulting from natural selection over millions of years. This means that humanity is neither the center nor the crown of creation but is only one of many species in the biosphere, all of them interdependent on the others. The notion that God fashioned us in His image is a prehistoric self-image of humanity that must be discarded because of the firmly established fact that evolution is accepted unanimously by the world's leading biologists.[4]

So certain is Wilson of the sweeping significance of Darwinism for both science and religion that he is dismayed by recent polls showing that half of Americans do not believe in evolution by natural selection or any other means. Instead, many campaign vigorously on behalf of theories such as Intelligent Design for which, as Wilson sees it, "there is no evidence, no theory, and no criteria for proof that even marginally might pass for science."[5] To counterattack this foolishness, he recently edited the four key books of Charles Darwin for republication in a single volume to which he contributed a general introduction and an afterword, contending for their enduring relevance despite the continuing attacks of religion.[6] Driving this unabashed advocacy of evolution is a passionate conviction that scientific humanism is "the only worldview compatible with science's growing knowledge of the real world and the laws of nature."[7]

Lest all of this sound like hostility toward religion by its cultured despisers, Wilson is quick to concede that faith once played an important role in human history. It gave us an inspiring religious epic, sponsored the arts, and fostered altruism by codifying our highest values as moral imperatives. Indeed, science was not ready to replace religion as the ultimate arbiter of reality until its methodology was established by the Enlightenment of the eighteenth century. But now that science has grasped the controlling clue of evolution by natural selection, it is time for religion to retire and give it full sway to secularize the human story. After all, what science claims that evolution was able to achieve by blind chance is every bit as amazing as what religion claims that God was able to achieve by divine creation.

I have sought in as few words as possible to present a fair and balanced summary of the views of a leading scientist in order to illustrate the depth of the challenge that religion faces in the contentious debate over evolution. But before we respond it may be well to let Wilson speak for himself:

> I had been raised a Southern Baptist, laid backward under the water on the sturdy arm of a pastor, been born again. I knew the healing power of redemption. Faith, hope, and charity were in my bones, and with millions of others I knew that my savior Jesus Christ would grant me eternal life . . . But now at college . . . I chose to doubt . . . most of all [because] Baptist theology made no provision for evolution. The biblical authors had missed the most important revelation of all! Could it be that they were really privy to the thoughts of God? Might the pastors of my childhood, good and loving men though they were, be mistaken? It was all too much, and freedom was ever so sweet. I drifted away from the church, not definitively agnostic or atheistic, just Baptist no more.[8]

The logic of Wilson is clear and, on his premises, compelling. He wants us to make a choice, as did he, between science and religion. Nor does he leave any doubt which, in his view, is the better option. If we wish to cling to religion as a relic of the past for purposes of social acceptance, he will understand our decision but regard it as riddled with contradictions. As well as anyone, Wilson forces us to face the gut issue in the evolution debate: are science and religion finally incompatible? His answer is an unequivocal yes while mine is a not-necessarily-so. There is opportunity here to deal only with three central presuppositions underlying his verdict, all of which, in my view, seriously misrepresent the Christian faith. To rethink these basic assumptions could open the door to more fruitful avenues of dialogue between long-time adversaries.

Top Down Religion vs. Bottom Up Science

The first is Wilson's formulation of the fundamental issue as a choice between the transcendentalism of religion and the empiricism of science. He uses these categories to contrast the two worldviews as belonging to opposing camps. Those in the former are idealists while those in the latter are realists. The former reason deductively from general principles while the latter reason inductively from specific facts. The former are supernaturalists who want to escape from this world while the latter are naturalists who want to care for this world. In religion, the chain of causation begins with *ought* and runs downward to make absolute claims based on commandments, while in science the chain of causation begins with *is* and runs upward to make relative choices based on innate feelings and historical experience. For the former, reality is ultimately spiritual while, for the latter, it is ultimately physical. So understood by Wilson, the stakes could not be higher. He states, "The choice between transcendentalism and empiricism will be the coming century's version of the struggle for men's souls."[9]

While some of these distinctions may be valid in other religions, they hardly capture the uniqueness of

Christianity. Jesus ministered to a people looking for their cherished hope of the Kingdom of God to come top-down in supernatural fashion from the heavens, but He taught that it would come mysteriously from below like the seed growing under their feet (Mark 4:1-34). The only way it could be observed was inductively, not in external signs and wonders but in the quality of relationships between His followers (Luke 17:20-21). By the time that the Gospel of John was written, Wilson's split between transcendentalism and empiricism had been overcome in the affirmation that the eternal Logos was embodied in a flesh-and-blood life that entered fully into the particularity of human existence (John 1:14). As John put it, the most transcendent realities in life were heard with our ears, seen with our eyes, and handled with our hands (1 John 1:1), which is about as empirical a claim as a first century writer could make. No wonder William Temple called Christianity "the most materialistic of all great religions."[10]

So I would counter that the Christian doctrine of incarnation overcomes the necessary dualism between spirit and matter central to Wilson's understanding.

Body vs. Soul

The second move that Wilson makes is to create an unbridgeable gap between body and soul, the former in the domain of science and the latter in the domain of religion. Thus if religious experiences as subjective as affection or mysticism can be given a biological explanation rooted in genetic history or brain circuitry, then science is entitled to claim them as its own. We have long known the impact of hormones such as testosterone on personality traits, but researchers are now suggesting that neurotransmitters such as dopamine, serotonin, and oxytocin are responsible for some of our deepest emotional attitudes.[11]

Obviously Wilson thinks that it is only a matter of time until science discovers a physical rather than a metaphysical explanation for everything that we feel, including even the religious impulse itself.[12] Would such an achievement give science an unqualified victory over religion, confirming the old retort that it's not God but our glands that prompt us to be pious? Consider for a moment the ancient biblical understanding of the self as a unity comprising both body and soul, rather than a duality setting the two in opposition, as does Wilson. According to the creation account (Genesis 2:7), we are not, as the Greeks supposed, an inward spiritual soul trapped in an outward physical body. Rather, we are, in the totality of our being, an indivisible body-soul so that all of our sensations, volitions, and cognitions belong to the whole.[13]

In that case it would be normal for the body to reflect the life of the spirit and, conversely, for the spirit to reflect the life of the body. Of course, Wilson might reject this ancient Hebrew psychology as nothing more than "Iron Age folk knowledge," but this wholistic understanding of the physical and spiritual aspects of life as profoundly integrating and reciprocating may point to what psychosomatic medicine is just beginning to teach us.[14] I would be neither surprised nor dismayed if one day science were able to show us that everything we experience in our spirit is implanted in our body and religion were able to show us that everything we experience in our body is implanted in our spirit.

Static Religion vs. Dynamic Science

A third dichotomy undergirding Wilson's position is his characterization of religion as static and of science as dynamic. As regards the former, its foundations are frozen in a collection of ancient scriptures that cannot be revised, replaced, or enlarged. The interpretation of these writings long ago hardened into dogma that must be accepted as taught by church authorities. The end result, especially for Baptists, is a fundamentalism that absolutizes the convictions of a few charismatic leaders on threat of exclusion: agree or get out. By contrast, science is a venture of unending discovery. Its every hypothesis must be rigorously tested and immediately discarded if not verified by objective research. This difference was evident in the long journey of Darwin himself. At the outset, he was "quite orthodox," often quoting the Bible to settle points of morality. But gradually he shed his blind faith, which, as Wilson puts it, "gave him the intellectual fearlessness to explore human evolution wherever logic and evidence took him."[15]

The problem is that this depiction misses the whole point of biblical religion. As regards creation, it began in Genesis as a gradual sequence in six stages and continued throughout the Old Testament as an unending struggle against chaos, causing Jesus to say, "My Father is working still, and I also am working" (John 5:17). That work will not be finished until the creation is "set free from its bondage to decay and obtain the glorious liberty of the children of God" (Romans 8:21). Indeed, the whole goal of biblical history is "a new heaven and a new earth" (Revelation 21:1) where the order and harmony of the physical realm will be in every way equal to that of the spiritual realm. As regards adherence to brittle dogma, there is no way to understand the prophets of the Old Testament, the Jesus of the Gospels, or the Paul of the Epistles without viewing them as radical reformers intent on shattering the religious status quo. As regards Baptist fundamentalism, it is a pity that the young Wilson left the Baptist fold before learning that our movement emerged out of the left wing of the Reformation as a cry for freedom from the strictures of the established church.

Comparing Apples to Apples

In seeking to overcome these three dualities in Wilson's argument, I am not attempting to correct his scientific views, which I am hardly competent to do, but rather to offer him a different understanding of religion, which lies at the heart of biblical faith. Without these corrections the debate is over before it begins. I have no interest in defending the kind of religion that he attacks. But if Wilson is open to consider the perspectives advanced here, the evidence for which is far more extensive than I could mention, then he might realize that there is a valid understanding of religion that is empirical, holistic, and dynamic in nature, which religion would not only permit but encourage the full exercise of his scientific genius. As matters now stand, Wilson has framed the issues in such a way that to be a good believer is, in the nature of the case, to be a bad scientist, which I am very sure is not the true scandal of the gospel.

Now that we have looked at how Wilson and I differ in a few crucial areas, it is time to ask why this should be the case. Wilson is a brilliant thinker with remarkably broad interests who has doubtless read more about religion than I have about science. And yet I cannot recognize my religion in what he has to say about Christianity in general or Baptists in particular. A primary reason, I think, is because the samples he selects for study in the two areas are not comparable.

As regards science, he limits himself to those biologists, like himself, who are "statured by the peer review and publication of substantial personal research on the subject in leading journals of science . . . ."[16] I would guess that there are several hundred thousand scientists in this country teaching in high schools, colleges, and universities or working in business, industry, and government, but that no more than 5,000 of them meet Wilson's definition of "statured." In other words, when he describes science, he is basing his observations on the views of a tightly controlled group of the brightest and best scholars in that discipline.

But when he talks about religion, no such selectivity is at work. While I would not say that he picks the worst possible examples of religious life, his highly generalized descriptions are typical of grass-roots folk religion that might fairly be called the lowest common denominator. In other words, when discussing science he talks about its providers but when discussing religion he talks about its consumers. But what if we leveled the playing field? There are more than 300,000 Christian clergy in America, some 5,000 of whom may meet Wilson's test of being "statured," most of them teaching in universities or theological schools. If Wilson limited his sample of theologians to that highly elitist group, as he does with scientists, a very different picture of religion would emerge, one far more compatible with science than his writings suggest.

Let me illustrate by choosing an example dear to Wilson's heart. One of the things that repulses him the most about religion is its destructive side, its tendency to demonize those who differ and resort to aggression in the name of God. Again and again he laments the union of religion and tribalism that gives birth to bigotry and violence. Indeed, he is not sure that a rapprochement between science and religion is either possible or desirable because "there is something deep in religious belief that divides people and amplifies societal conflict."[17] As best I can tell, that sweeping generalization does not describe a single member of the American Academy of Religion, the closest counterpart to Wilson's "statured" scientists. Instead, the leaders of religion are united in condemning and combating every form of religious aggression, as Wilson could easily verify by stepping next door to observe the work of the Harvard Divinity School faculty.[18]

The point, of course, is that any great human endeavor can be easily hijacked, especially a voluntary movement like religion in a country where freedom of belief is so jealously guarded. I deplore the corruption of religion every bit as much as Wilson does and have spent as many years as he has seeking to expose those who would manipulate it for unworthy purposes. But it does not help to be told that the problem is with my religion rather than with those false shepherds who break in to fleece the sheep (Ezekiel 34:1-16; John 10:7-18). After all, science can be hijacked as well. Scientists split the atom to unleash nuclear energy, but I do not condemn them for incinerating whole cities. Scientists developed the chemicals and pesticides needed by modern industry and agriculture, but I do not blame them for poisoning so many of our waterways. Some scientists compromised their objectivity in accepting lavish funding for their research from major pharmaceutical companies, but I do not stereotype all scientists as pawns of big business. There will always be charlatans in the laboratory as well as in the pulpit, as the recent scandal over cloning in South Korea illustrates. The need is not for science and religion to find fault with each other but for both to do everything possible to keep their respective houses in order so as to offer their best for the benefit of the other.

To that end, what can we do to make our church a more welcoming place for scientists? We can begin by cultivating a faith unafraid of fact; a faith willing to think, to question, even to doubt; a faith that does not have all of the answers but is trying to ask the right questions. We can recover a robust doctrine of creation that celebrates each new discovery of its wondrous workings and mandates its perpetual care as a fit habitat for all that lives upon it. We can rid our relationships of any hint of smug self-satisfaction that assumes that we are always right and that those who differ are enemies worthy of our contempt. We can call forth our best minds to be trained as learned interpreters of both science and religion, knowing that the issues which they pose are not well handled by intellectual laggards. In short, we can take science seriously, paying attention to its findings, cheering its discoveries, supporting its progress.

Christ: The Ultimate Source of Consilience

This being a Baptist sermon nearing its end, Wilson would know only too well what comes next: the invitation.[19] Nor do we need to be diffident about appealing for decision. One thing that Wilson carried over into science from religion was its evangelistic fervor. Whenever I read his books or hear him speak I am keenly aware that he is trying to convert me to his position. It will not embarrass him to learn that I would like to have him on my side just as much as he would like to have me on his side. His rejection of the religion of his youth does not make him my enemy or even my adversary. Rather, he is to me a lovely and lovable human being with an incredible capacity to appreciate the creativity lurking in life all about us. I cannot think of anyone with whom I would rather stand in these pews and sing a grand old hymn of the faith or chat with after a church dinner about how to live authentically in our crazy kind of world.

But has Wilson strayed so far from the fold that there is no longer any point of contact from which to urge a reconsideration of his avowed secularism? I think not. After more than sixty years he still cannot forget his adolescent flirtation with faith but recounts it in his most recent writings.[20] As I read between the lines it is hard not to sense a stifled yearning for grace. For example, in January 1984, he tells how he was invited by "an old friend with similar Southern Baptist background" to attend a service at Harvard conducted by Martin Luther King, Sr. When the father of the slain civil rights leader finished his homily, "subterranean feelings surfaced without warning" as "a choir of black Harvard students surprised me by singing a medley of old-time gospel hymns, with a professionalism equaling anything I ever heard in the churches of my youth. To my even greater surprise, I wept quietly as I listened. My people, I thought. My people. And what else lay hidden deep within my soul?"[21]

In our Scripture lesson this morning (Colossians 1:15-20), Paul addresses a young church struggling with science and religion: how to relate the world around them to the faith within them. His response was that Christ reconciles the realms of creation and redemption. He is both the creator who gave life to all things (v. 16) and the created who made the invisible God visible here on earth (v. 15). To say that "all things" were created in Him, through Him, and for Him was Paul's way of claiming that Christ gives meaning to our involvement with everything that is. Because of this, in Christ "all things cohere" (v. 17) or, to use Wilson's word, find their "consilience." When neither religion nor science triumphs but Christ is made "preeminent" (v. 18), we may embrace the whole of reality, whether physical or spiritual, and discover the kind of life that is supremely worth living.

Expanded version of a sermon preached in the Mountain Brook Baptist Church, Birmingham, Alabama, March 19, 2006.

Article reprinted from *Christian Ethics Today*, vol. 12, no. 3, (Summer 2006), 9-13. Used with permission. http://www.christianethicstoday. com/cetart/index.cfm?fuseaction=Articles.main&ArtID=1406.

References:

[1]   Wilson recounts his spiritual odyssey in the memoir *Naturalist* (Washington: Island Press, 1994), 33-46. He made a profession of faith at age fourteen at First Baptist Church, Pensacola, Florida, and was baptized in February 1944, by its pastor, Dr. Wallace Rogers, who became a friend of mine many years later during his ministry in Charleston, South Carolina.

²   On the sensationalistic "monkey trial" pitting William Jennings Bryan against Clarence Darrow see Edward J. Larson, *Summer for the Gods: The Scopes Trial and America's Continuing Debate Over Science and Religion* (New York: Basic Books, 1997).

³   Edward O. Wilson, *Consilience: The Unity of Knowledge* (New York: Alfred A. Knopf, 1999), 297.

⁴   For a convenient summary of Wilson's views on Darwinism, see his "Intelligent Evolution," *Harvard Magazine,* November-December, 2005, 29-33.

⁵   Edward Wilson, "Intelligent Evolution," 31.

⁶   Edward O. Wilson, ed., *From So Simple a Beginning: The Four Great Books of Charles Darwin* (New York: W. W. Norton, 2005). The article cited in note 5 is a reprint of the essays by Wilson for this volume. The four books of Darwin included here are *Voyage of the Beagle* (1845), *On the Origin of Species* (1859), *The Descent of Man* (1871), and *The Expression of the Emotions in Man and Animals* (1872).

⁷   Edward Wilson, "Intelligent Evolution," 33.

⁸   Edward Wilson, *Consilience,* 6.

⁹   Edward Wilson, *Consilience,* 240.

¹⁰   William Temple, *Readings in St. John's Gospel* (London: Macmillan, 1959), xx.

¹¹   For recent popular reports see Lauren Slater, "True Love," *National Geographic* (February 2006), 32-49; Lori Gottlieb, "How Do I Love Thee?" *Atlantic Monthly* (March 2006), 58-70.

¹²   For an evolutionary approach to religion see Paul Bloom, "Is God an Accident?" *Atlantic Monthly* (December 2005), 105-12.

¹³   A detailed exposition of Hebrew anthropology was worked out by Johannes Pedersen, *Israel: Its Life and Culture,* I-II (London: Geoffrey Cumberlege, 1926), 99-181.

[14]   Edward Wilson, *Consilience,* 269.

[15]   Edward Wilson, "Intelligent Evolution," 33.

[16]   Edward Wilson, "Intelligent Evolution," 31.

[17]   Edward Wilson, "Intelligent Evolution," 33.

[18]   The most historic building of the Harvard Divinity School is Divinity Hall where Ralph Waldo Emerson delivered his famous 1838 commencement address. Interestingly enough, it is surrounded by buildings well known to Wilson: the Museum of Comparative Zoology, the Bauer Center for Genomics Research, the University Herbaria, and the Biological Laboratories of the Department of Molecular and Cellular Biology.

[19]   Wilson begins the chapter of his memoir on childhood religion with a vivid description of "the Invitation" to which he responded in January 1944. See *Naturalist,* 33-36.

[20]   Typical is the way that he inserted this theme into the opening pages of *Consilience,* 5-6. Wilson wanted to title his next book *The Creation: Letter to a Southern Baptist Pastor* but finally decided on *The Creation: A Meeting of Science and Religion.*

[21]   Edward Wilson, *Naturalist,* 45-46. I hope that it will not be viewed as special pleading for me to wonder if more than brain circuitry was the cause of those tears.

Editor's Note:

Following a distinguished career in the pastorate and professoriate, Calvin Miller serves as Research Professor and Distinguished Writer in Residence at Samford's Beeson Divinity School. A prolific writer of more than forty books, Miller honors Tom with an essay on books for this volume. Anyone who knew Tom well knew of his intense love affair with books – old books, leather-bound books, and specially bound or decorated books. He loved the content too and was a voracious and eclectic reader throughout his adult life and authored several volumes himself in his latter years. Brother Tom would surely resonate with Miller's creative and artful lament in this chapter.

CHAPTER 9

THE WRITING PROFESSOR: THE FATE OF ACADEMIC PRINT IN THE AGE OF IMAGE

By Calvin Miller

In the middle of the twentieth century, there came a vast shifting of communication paradigms. The thing that most captured my imagination was that this shift was never proclaimed or divined by philosophers. It just happened. Every anthropological guru or pundit seemed to agree that the shift was occurring without ever colluding to bring it about. Historians from Barbara Tuchman to Thomas Cahill agreed that it happened and their work added to the long, long columns of print that twisted through the closing decades of the twentieth century.

But this age of change named itself differently than we thought it would.

I was a boy nine years of age when the bombs fell

on Hiroshima and Nagasaki. This horrendous finale to World War II at first was named the era of the Nuclear Age or the Atomic Age. This title seemed ominous with a hint of Armageddon about it. In fact when Douglas McArthur presided over the Japanese surrender from the decks of the Battleship Missouri, he actually used the word "Armageddon" in his speech:

> ... Military alliances, balances of power, leagues of nations, all in turn failed, leaving the only path to be by way of the crucible of war. We have had our last chance. If we do not now devise some greater and more equitable system, Armageddon will be at our door. The problem basically is theological and involves a spiritual recrudescence and improvement of human character that will synchronize with our almost matchless advances in science, art, literature and all material and cultural development of the past two thousand years. It must be of the spirit if we are to save the flesh.[1]

It was natural to assume that everything following McArthur's speech would be post-apocalyptic. This doomsday tone naturally led us, the children of the Apocalypse, to refer to the new paradigm as the Nuclear Age. But not a lot of time elapsed before this fearsome title began to be replaced by the term the Communication Age.

Alvin Toffler called the entirety of world history up to 1750 *The First Wave*. He renamed the Industrial Age, 1750-1950, *The Second Wave*. Finally he called this new post-1950 age *The Third Wave*, defining it roughly as the communication age. Jeremy Rifkin called it *The*

Emerging Order. Barbara Tuchman referred to the age as a return of the fourteenth century's *Distant Mirror.* It was a "hinge of history," she said. On and on the books seeking a definition for the age continued to flow. Christopher Lasch, by the end of the twentieth century, explored *The New Narcissism.* Ernie Becker wrote *The Denial of Death.* And more recently, Thomas Friedman wrote *The World is Flat,* a book out of which I will shortly quote. The one thing all these books have in common is their diagnostic. All of them agree that the post-1950 world was somehow new and different. Further, all of them presumed that the thing that was vastly different in this post-apocalyptic world was the birth of this new communication paradigm. No two of them called it the same thing, but none of them seemed to miss the point that the world was being re-born into a new mode: the communication age.

     Since it seems that we have all universally agreed that our age is the age of communication, we must ask, "What is the elemental nature of this new form of communication?" At its heart it is digital communication. As printing marked forever the way we view the fourteenth century, so the computer will forever mark the way we view the twentieth. Neal Postman in his 1985 book, *Amusing Ourselves to Death,* agreed that we had left the world of typography, the world of the printing press, behind. Postman called this new post-printing age *The Age of Exposition:*

> Almost all of the characteristics we associate
> with mature discourse were amplified by
> typography, which has the strongest possible
> bias toward exposition: a sophisticated
> ability to think conceptually, deductively
> and sequentially; a high valuation of reading
> and order; an abhorrence of contradiction;

a large capacity for detachment and objectivity; and a tolerance for delayed response. Toward the end of the nineteenth century for reasons I am most anxious to explain, the age of exposition began to pass, and the early signs of its displacement could be discerned. Its replacement was to be the Age of Show Business.[2]

I do not want to confuse you with whether or not Postman's *Age of Show Business* is equivalent to the age of communication in general or the age of the computer in particular, but I must point out that both conceptions of the age have been seen as an age of lazy-mindedness that moved the world away from paper books and toward e-books. The age of communication was marked by an explosion of knowledge and paradoxically, at the same time, was characterized as a dumb down epoch. Even Postman would have to concede that the Age of Show Business, the birth of the Age of Entertainment, thrived on the sort of entertainment that had to be picked up from the glassy face of the great digitized image maker: the computer monitor.

"Let Me Entertain You," however, is the most common elevator music of the digital age. Further, the average nineteen-year-old boy in America is not the most avid reader of paper books, but he is setting the standard for what goes on at the cinema in the entertainment world. The average nineteen-year-old boy is seeing thirty-three movies for every book he reads. This is where Neal Postman's Age of Entertainment and the Age of Communication pass close. Further, this nineteen-year-old, sub scholar, is generally a techie wizard, moving in and out of his cyber-world with an ease that most scholars wish they owned. He is not a good reader (at least the reading of paper books), but he loves monitor screens, and understands perfectly what he wants to know and needs to know from the electronic print that comes to him in minimal amounts while he clutches a Classic Coca-Cola in one hand and a Mac mouse in the other.

So much for paradigm shifts and the dying world of paper books.

So what about those publish-or-perish questions that have long absorbed professors? There are three questions I want to answer in these critical days of academic publishing and the death of paper books. First, can older professors really ever accept the brave new world of digitized books? Can they really love the e-libraries of that world and live without the mystical romance of their armchairs, pipe tobacco, and paper books? Second, since it is getting harder and harder to find a credible publisher to print our academic books, should we be open to self-publishing? Is self-publishing our own opinion articles and text books a good thing, or is it merely an unnecessary and ego-driven attempt to arrive at self-esteem? Third, is cyber-scholarship really more creative than pen and paper ideation? Let us look at these critical issues, one at a time.

Can Professors Live Without the Romance of Armchairs, Pipe Tobacco, and Paper Books?

If you are like I am – seventy-four years of age and wistfully in love with print – you know what I mean when I say my books are my friends. Book-friends, like people-friends, are eclectic and hard to categorize. Some are old and wise and counselors to my need. These books are heavy with information that informs and then transforms our lives. Some books are quirky, bothersome, and dull. It is hard to spend more than a few minutes with dull books before their lightsome, chatty naiveté drives us up a tree. Some books are light and frothy. These books are untried, written by people who are untried. Some are operating on half a brain, others on half a heart. Some I only read a few paragraphs before I take them to a charity donation center, even though I feel guilty giving a bad book away, because it may contribute to polluting the world.

But at the outset let me say if you feel romantically toward books, you have been born into a cold and romance-less age. It is easy to snuggle up to a dog-eared, 500-page lover, whose pages coo into your weariness. But a plasma or LCD screen? Not a chance! There is a cold matter-of-factness about the scholarship you dig out of your hard drive. And most of us would agree with the savant who said, "Paper books are the souvenirs of the way we felt."

Even the great poets seem colder when read from a computer screen than from a smudged page. It is not my intention to make a defense of paper books. But it almost seems to me that Samuel Taylor Coleridge was seeing down a long, plasma corridor of our glassy- faced computers when he wrote:

> In Xanadu . . . did Kubla Khan
> A stately pleasure dome decree:
> Where Alph the sacred river, ran
> Through caverns measureless to man
> Down to a sunless sea.

The bland and unmeasured caverns of cold binary systems hearken to darkened rooms, sunless seas. Long ago I thought Lord Alfred Tennyson's prophecies were of mere flight and rocketry, but now I think his *Locksley Hall*

prophecies might equally be stated as a kind of vision of
our volatile, virtual world:

> For I dipped into the future, far as
> human eye could see,
> > Saw the vision of the world, and all the
> > wonder that would be;
> > > Saw the heavens filled with
> > > commerce, argosies of magic sails,
> > > > Pilots of the purple twilight,
> > > > dripping down with costly bales . . .

The heavens it seems are filled with commerce,
down to the tiny BlackBerrys, iPhones, iPads, and various
droids that allow us access to Wall Street in the push of
our personal business. But more than that, everything
is reduced to commerce. The word "enter" brings up a
poem of Ovid as easily as it does the Dow Jones Industrial
Average.

Interpret as you like, but computers reduce
everything to transaction. Over the years I have owned
possibly twenty different computers. Where are they now?
In cyber-graveyards, taking their mummified hard drives
with them. The truth is I have never developed a love
affair with any of them. As a matter of fact, I have hated
nearly all of them from time to time. I have shrieked at
them when they have lost whole chapters of a book that
I have had to re-create completely from scratch. I have
taken them to the electronics store nerds to operate on
their innards so they could try to replace the lost glory
of an idea I foolishly trusted to Silicon Valley science.
No love lost there. The only affection I have ever felt for
computers, and only for a moment, was when they were
new and obedient and communicating with their Wi-Fi
printers.

But with my books, it is never so. I have never taken any illicit human lover to bed but oh, I have taken a well-written book, my mistress in print, to bed, unable to leave her in the armchair. She is a warm companion who will not forsake me when "we get behind closed doors." We have tumbled into bed together, she and I, as I explore her enticing pages. My books all seem to know they are one of my literary concubines. When I turn on the light in my library at bedtime this harem of shelved sirens smiles, each of them crying, choose me tonight. Cuddle me, write on my pages, drool in fascination, I am yours. Of *course* I prefer paper books to my computer. When I drool into my keyboard, it shorts out.

But now, I encourage you. Never mistreat your books. As for your computer, do what you will. Show it no kindness. It will not stick with you for long. It holds nothing of interest in its tiny binary processor. It is all ones and zeroes. It is nothing more than a motherboard of transistors and microchips. What does it know of life and love and tears? Still, as a scholar you are destined to live with this cold devil. She keeps your world of memory survival locked in her innards. You dare not cast this medusa out, or your mind will turn to stone. This hateful hag is no warm lover, but unfortunately she keeps your mind in her box.

Get a grip on your attitude. The great divorce has come. Your life has been changed by people like Hewlett and Packard, Gates, Jobs, and Dell. The world you so despise is the only one left to you. Whatsoever you desire must now be "Kindled" by Kindle. If you want to survive, burn your library card and push the "ON" button.

Is Self-Publishing Our Own Opinions and Text Books a Good Thing?

Self-publishing has been going on for a long time. Thoreau could not get his first book, *The Concord and the Merrimac*, published, so he decided to publish it himself in the amount of 1,000 copies. It was not a runaway best seller. Four years later the publisher returned 706 of the yet unsold volumes to the author. It had to hurt a bit, but that night Thoreau wrote in his journal, "I now have more than 900 books in my library, 706 of which I have written myself."

Should professors be their own publishers? One such press, Professor Textbook, advertises: "Your Textbook – Your Way." The idea behind this web-based publishing company is that you can "publish your own textbook, built from your own original material, and customized for your course," giving you control over your own learning environments.[3] In a way the business makes sense. Why? Because it is getting harder and harder for professors to get published in the traditional way.

Three things are affecting the book market. First of all we live in a dumb down culture, in part made dumb down by the diminishing presence of paper books in the marketplace. Motoko Rich wrote in the *New York Times*:

The point may soon come when there are more people who want to write books than there are people who want to read them. At least, that is what the evidence suggests. Booksellers, hobbled by the economic crisis, are struggling to lure readers. Almost all the New York publishing houses are laying off editors and pinching pennies. Small bookstores are closing. Big chains are

laying people off or exploring bankruptcy
. . . As traditional publishers look to prune
their booklists and rely increasingly on
blockbuster best sellers, they are ramping
up their title counts (with self-published
titles) and making money on books that
sell as few as five copies . . . Eileen Gittins is
chief executive of Blurb, a print-on-demand
company, whose revenue has grown from $1
million to $30 million in only two years. . .
published 300,000 titles last year. Many of
those were personal books bought only by
the author.[4]

But there is something to be said about professors
making their own lectures and text notes into books
that exactly fit their teaching style and schedule. The
only caveat that needs to be sounded is this: beware the
economics of self-publishing.

I have been among those few and fortunate
professors who have managed to get all their textbooks
published in the traditional way: the way that pays you
advances and royalties with no money spent out of one's
own pocket. This has the extra advantage of seeing one's
own textbook at use in many other schools, and there is,
of course, a sense of reward in that as well. But had it not
been so, I am almost sure I would have self-published my
own textbooks, simply because I like the feel of having my
books and lectures written in a common mind.

I am not the only one who feels this way. David
Gessner in a separate *New York Times* article said:

Though I sometimes chafe at my collar,
just as often I appreciate the miracle of the
job. A typical, creative writing professor has

four months of summer vacation; teaches
passionate young people a subject they
actually want to learn about (and often
enjoy); carries a light two-class load per
term that is the envy of professors in other
departments; and gains both a sense of
belonging and ego satisfaction as a pillar
– even a star – of an intense community of
writers and readers. Furthermore, in a time
when it is increasingly difficult for literary
writers to support themselves through their
writing, professorships provide an attractive
alternative to working as a bookstore clerk,
carpenter's helper or a busboy.[5]

In the same article, Gessner, like most of us, was
terribly impressed with Wallace Stegner. Of Stegner's
genius and ingenuity Gessner remarked, "A product of
the depression, he solved the great and ever-pressing
economic question of the writing life with a simple answer.
He got a job."[6] And of course that job was teaching. Most
of us who write could not always make a living just by
teaching but we found Stegner's way out. We chose a life
that made both our writing and our teaching join hands.
Inevitably we came to see that both our readers and our
students (and they are sometimes one and the same) were
better off for our double life.

Motoko Rich speaks to that deep-seated drive that
all of us who teach have – we want to publish. "Anyway,
even if you're sitting at a dinner party, if you ask how many
people want to write a book, everyone will say, 'I've got a
book or two in me,' said Kevin Weiss, chief executive of
Author Solutions. 'We don't see a let up in the number
of people who are interested in writing.'"[7] This is true

of most professors. The purpose of most professors who have *light-load tenures* is to foster the publish-rather-than-perish option. Professors are the best possible source of self-publishing, and when Alfred A. Knopf says "no," a professor can, like the little red hen say, "Then I will do it myself."

Is Cyber Scholarship Really More Creative than Paper Book Creativity?

Self-publishing is but one answer to the writing professor's dilemma. Whole libraries are now being digitized at the rate of 10 million titles per year by Google alone. This is all the more remarkable when you realize that there are said to be no more than 65 million English titles in print. Digitizing at this rate would put nearly all books in digital form over the next few years. Berkeley's Library alone has stipulated their goal is to digitize 3,000 books per week. What this craze means is that entire libraries are about to be replaced by e-libraries. Paper books in time it seems are due to be displaced by digitized replicas, read only by way of various downloading and scanning devices. Massive efforts have transformed many thousands of books into digitized titles ready to be downloaded onto their electronic reading pads. Given the current digitizing craze, the definition of both writing and books must be re-examined. The modern professor will have to ask, "What is a book" and certainly "What does it mean to be published."[8]

Yes! That's the question: What exactly does it mean to publish academic books and papers when the word "book" for many really means a digital file and the word "paper" literally means a binary storage item. Not only is the romance of book reading gone, but the writer's self-esteem is greatly diminished by the loss of being able to say, "See, this book is mine. I did this. I wrote this. Oh, you have my *book*... my beautiful paper book... would you like me to sign *your* book... I mean, *my* book."

No wonder Ted Nelson wrote this for the Oxford Internet Institute:

> The original hypertext concept from the 1960s was to replace paper with something far better – a sweeping new literary genre subsuming all previous forms of writing and publication showing connections that were previously invisible and enabling connections that were previously impossible, all in cinematic, swooping new visualizations. We would see and manipulate not just pages, but new units and forms – streamers, tunnels, fountains and cataracts of texts that could be poured, stretched and zoomed. All of this would be fluidly reusable and incrementally perishable, facilitating scholarly commentary and dissent, education without subject boundaries, work without deadlines.
>
> Instead, today's computer world is stilted, clumsy and traditional, based on awkward interactions designed by techies in the 70s. Today's world of digital documents has frozen into the simulation of paper – but worse than paper: paper under glass that you cannot even annotate; forced into hierarchical structures, and pre-categorized for all time... We foresaw worldwide,

anarchic hypertext publishing, others think
the World Wide Web is the fulfillment of our
dream, as well as a miracle of enlightenment.
I see it as the dismal dumb-down of what
could and still may be.[9]

Nelson is definitely right in linking the digitizing
of books to the dumbing down of the society. The writing
professor, like every other dedicated reader, will have
to ask, "What happens to me when I can no longer get
anything published because the kind of publishing I
understand is no longer available to me? Can I go from
digitized notes to digitized books, without ever the
necessity of print?" I predict that younger professors will be
better able to make the change than older ones.

But the important warning that should be sounded
is this: Is the endless cyber-forest a place of creativity? Most
people like Ted Nelson would say probably not. Thomas
Friedman castigates all notions that the techie crowd has
created greater national creativity. In summing up the
entire virtual world, he cleverly called his magnificent
book *The World is Flat*. And what has flattened it? The
geeks and nerds and all those better-adjusted people they
are leading through the world with a virtual rope. With
nerds and geeks as our instructors, it is likely that we
will all become nerds and geeks. Then we will know that
Friedman is right: the world *is* flat.

Michael Arguello emphasized the world's flat
state in an email he sent to Thomas Friedman when he
wrote, "I taught at a local university. It was disheartening
to see the poor work ethic of many of my students. Of
the students I taught over six semesters, I'd only consider
hiring two of them. The rest lacked the creativity, problem-
solving abilities and passion for learning."[10] In fact, both

Arguello and Friedman agree that the brightest students on American campuses are foreign students. "The Indians that I work with are the cream of the crop. They are educated by the equivalents of MIT back in India and there are plenty of them."[11] But if the Indians and Chinese are "smarting up," the dismal evidence remains that American students are dumbing down – in spite of spending all their lives in front of computer screens.

On December 16, 2005, the *New York Times* carried a story reporting that the average American college graduate's literacy in English had declined significantly over the past decade, according to a widely respected nationwide test. This refers to college graduates – not dropouts. The *Times* article stated:

> The National Assessment of Adult Literacy, given in 2003 by the Department of Education, is the most important test of how well Americans can read. The test also found steep declines in the English literacy of Hispanics, and significant increases among blacks and Asians. When the last test was administered in 1992, 40% of the nation's college graduates scored at the proficient level, meaning that they were able to read lengthy, complex English texts and draw complicated inferences. But on the 2003 test, only 31% of the graduates demonstrated those high level skills . . . Grover J. Whitehurst, director of the institute within the Department of Education that helped to oversee the test, said that he believed that the literacy of college graduates had dropped because a rising number of young Americans in recent years had spent their

free time watching television or surfing the
Internet. 'We're seeing significant declines
in reading for pleasure, and its showing up
in our literacy levels,' he said.'[12]

From Friedman's research we can infer that not
only does computer literacy not contribute to creativity, it
also varies inversely with the dumbing down of America.

Conclusion

How does all this figure into the milieu of the
writing professor? In this way: Not only is it harder and
harder to get paper book research into paper book print,
but it is ever so much harder to see an advance in the
quality of students we are producing. We are in a cul-de-sac
of computer addiction that is wiping out to some degree
our best selves.

Let us agree then with these three facts. First of
all, we who teach should commit ourselves to writing
and publishing our own books, whether or not these are
paper or virtual books. Writing is the best way to leave
behind us our own personal legacy of thought and creative
reasoning. Second, publishing is still possible, even if it
means we self-publish. If this self-publishing is in the paper
realm, we have the double advantage of handling it in that
old-fashioned way that builds a romance around ourselves
and our world, and, frankly, it feels good. Third, books
are to a writer what paintings are to an artist. So much art
also is computer created. My grandson is a great artist,
and much of what he does in movie story boards or even
book covers is done right on the computer, but to me it
really never succeeds until I hold his pictures in my hand

or hang them on my wall. There's the trophy. And when I behold the trophy, I understand what Ayn Rand meant when she said, "Art is man defining himself."

I have now published more than forty books. Each of them was submitted to a publisher with the high hope of changing the world in some way. The entire collection stands on a shelf, in a special place, in our home. Each of these books helps circumscribe my sojourn in the world. When I pass that shelf I say to myself, "These are here because I taught and I wrote." In my last few years of writing, the computer screen loomed large above my effort. Many of my paper books have now become e-books, and I am grateful, but the truth is before they were digitized into e-books, they were plain old "b, s, and t" (blood, sweat, and tears) books. And it was in creating them in their pre-digitized form that I grew as a scholar.

I'm an old curmudgeon and I don't really care if people see me as such. Settling down into an armchair, with coffee dribbling down onto a good paper book, would be one of my favorite ways to die. It would at least be as good as "shuffling off this mortal coil" with a mouse in my hand, trying to find the right font for whatever flat-screen paragraph I am trying to finish.

Coleridge must have known:

> *That Alph, that sacred river, ran*
> *Through caverns measureless to man,*
> *Down to a sunless sea.*

That sunless sea must surely be the local e-library, where automatons clutch computer mice in some attempt to find their souls. Never really reading whole e-books, many of the scanners were only snippers, snipping their way into a partial life where you substitute scanning for actual reading. It is indeed for most student cyborgs a sunless sea.

But there is hope: the writing professor.

References:

[1] Douglas MacArthur, "Surrender ceremony on the U.S.S. Missouri," accessed August 24, 2011, www.pbs.org/wgbh/amex/macarthur/filmmore/reference/primary/macspeech04.html.

[2] Neal Postman, *Amusing Ourselves to Death* (New York: Penguin, 1985) p. 63.

[3] Professor Textbook, accessed August 24, 2011, www.ProfessorTextbook.com.

[4] Mokoto Rich, "Self Publishers Flourish as Writers Pay the Tab," *New York Times*, January 27, 2009. Parenthetical comments are mine.

[5] David Gessner, "Those Who Write, Teach," *New York Times*, Sept. 18, 2008.

[6] Ibid.

[7] Motoko Rich, "Self Publishers."

[8] An excerpt from *The Economist*, as quoted in the Global Technology Forum Newsletter.

[9] Ted Nelson, OH Fellow, "Hypertext and the Future of Literature," Oxford Internet Institute, 1 St. Giles, Oxford, OX13JS.

[10] Thomas L. Friedman, *The World is Flat* (New York: Farrar, Straus and Giroux, 2005), 341.

[11] Ibid.

[12] Ibid., 339-340.

Editor's Note:

J. I. Packer spoke on January 31, 2009, at a national meeting of the Council for Christian Colleges & Universities about "being an adult catechist." My brother, Tom, died just a few days later on February 4, 2009. As I reflected on Packer's commentary, his remarks resonated with me about my brother's life. Tom was a gifted speaker and in almost any setting or topic he was sharing openly or more subtly a distinctly Christian teaching. Tom studied Latin, and the Latin for "catechist" is catechista – to give oral instruction in Christianity by putting forth questions to arrive at answers. I was pleased that J.I. Packer happily permitted me to publish his talk in this memorial book.

CHAPTER 10

KINGDOM EDUCATION: TODAY'S TASK

By J. I. Packer

Captatio Lectoris

The basis of this address is that we are all at one in embracing the task of Christian higher education and that we share a common purpose of exploring its many perspectives and angles for the furthering of the Kingdom of God. The task is a massive one, and I had better begin by admitting that as a would-be educator myself, one who has been blessed with a longish and fairly settled life, I am saddened that I have not majored to better effect in this field. Like George Whitefield towards the end of his evangelistic ministry, I find myself moved to pray, "Lord, help me to begin to begin." The present occasion, however [the Awards Banquet at the Council for Christian Colleges

& Universities Presidents Conference], at least gives me opportunity to wave this torch I have tried to carry and try to pass it on, and that is what I shall now attempt to do.

The letter of invitation that brought me here told me, "We would like you to share your thoughts on being recognized as a leader in the Christian faith and talk about your years of serving as a pastor, theologian, and academic leader." My remarks will, I hope, go some way to fulfilling that agenda.

An Adult Catechist

A moment ago I identified myself as an educator. That, first and foremost, is what I take myself to be. An Englishman by extraction, a Canadian by choice, and in some circles an honorary American into the bargain, I have taught theology at Regent College, Vancouver, since 1979, and before that I had fourteen years' experience teaching the faith in English theological seminaries. Now technically retired, I hope to go on teaching as long as each year's classes give me tolerable course evaluations. I suppose it is natural, given this history, for people to typecast me as a theologian and stop there. However, when Alister McGrath wrote a theological narrative of my first seventy years, he said something slightly different. He hesitated to call me a theologian, because the ongoing in-house, or perhaps I should say, in-common-room, debates within the theologians' professional guild were so clearly not my main focus. He opted instead for labeling me a theologizer, one who knows and shows how to engage theologically with his peers even though he himself does not do very much of it, just because he is absorbed in doing something else. [1] I think McGrath was right; my vocational trajectory has not been primarily academic (though I have tried to be academically responsible in everything I have tackled). My central concerns have been churchly and pastoral, and nowadays, if asked what sort of educator I am, my reply is that I am seeking to fulfill the almost forgotten role of an adult catechist. Let me explain.

What is an adult catechist? He is one who practices what from the second to the fifth centuries, and then through the Reformation era, and still today in Roman Catholic and Orthodox circles, has been and is called *catechesis*: namely, instruction, angled for all ages and given at all levels of depth and detail, in two things that belong inseparably together – the truths by which Christians live and the discipline of living by them. Catechists labor to fulfill the twofold task that the Pastoral Epistles prioritize so insistently: that is, teaching people gospel truth and training them in gospel godliness. Today, as in the days of Christianity's spread throughout the Greco-Roman world, the need for catechesis is urgent, because the non-Christian society that surrounds the church is rife with alternative beliefs, both religious and anti-religious, that seem to rule out Christian faith from the start, or at least to subject it to ruinous distortion. Thus, while post-Christianity shouts loud, syncretism rides high, calling on us to affirm the transcendental unity of religions in some form and to mute our witness to the Trinity, the incarnation, the atonement, the resurrection, the reign and future return of the Lord Jesus Christ – in other words, to eliminate the Christian essentials altogether. This syncretism constitutes grand-scale heresy, indeed apostasy, and must be challenged and fought wherever it raises its head. Part of the needed counter to it must surely be the recovery of a catechumenate corresponding to that of earlier centuries – that is, a sustained pattern of ongoing instruction in orthodoxy and orthopraxy for the directing of outsiders, the reinvigorating of insiders, and the preparing of adults for baptism, along with the noting and correcting of errors that lure people away from authentic revealed truth. I identify all persons, clergy and laity, speakers and writers, members of church staffs and agents of parachurch ministries, who give themselves to this form of service as adult catechists and count myself among their number.

The catechizing of children and young people, both in church and at home, as has been attempted in most evangelical circles during the past half millennium, is a major part of the catechetical ministry for which the Bible calls, but it is not the whole of it. Catechizing should be seen as a discipline and program of lifelong teaching and learning designed in the first instance for the adults who constitute, or at least travel with, each local church, and shaped whenever possible as a family venture, as the Puritan Richard Baxter famously wanted it to be. [2]

Multiple methods are here in order; question and answer, presentation and discussion, shared study of books, surveying controversies that bear on the gospel, and exploring one's own tradition of Christian understanding and liturgical and corporate life, are all appropriate forms of catechetical nurture. As in our time evangelical congregations have been learning, or re-learning, the necessity of regular Bible reading and exposition for spiritual health, so now it seems to me overdue and urgent that we establish, or recover, catechetical education everywhere as needed for spiritual growth. Personally, in all my public ministry and published material over fifty years I have tried to work to this formula, that is, to proclaim Christian orthodoxy linked with practical Christian living, and it is on this basis that I proclaim myself an adult catechist before I am anything else.

You asked me to reflect on my service as a pastor. Not all adult catechists are pastors, of course, but I maintain that no one who is not an adult catechist can truly fulfill the pastor's role. I take that role to have three aspects. The pastor's job, as I see it, is to build up the people of God entrusted to his (or her) care, first, by promoting the Christian formation of their minds, where all aspects of discipleship are ultimately rooted; second, by promoting the Christian formation of their characters, in which the moral and spiritual image of Jesus Christ, their living Lord, should constantly be reflected; and third, by helping them use their God-given abilities of whatever kind, in imaginative, enterprising, loving service of others, according to the needs that they discern. And the way to induce advance in this threefold development of people's life-pattern, in while none of the changes occurs spontaneously and all encounter opposition, is to observe the maxim that I first heard spoken sixty years ago and that echoes in my ears still: namely, the maxim that one's three priorities in pastoral ministry are, first, to teach, and second, to teach, and third, to teach.

Vocationally, I do in fact view myself as a pastor, with both my adult catechetical ministry and my academic endeavors fitting into this frame, and for the past forty years I have been a supernumerary member of a local church's pastoral staff, in addition to my salaried occupation as a teacher of theology. Academically, I have one or two specialty areas in historical theology, but essentially I have settled for the identity of a generalist, one, that is, who takes into his purview as far as he can the full range of mainstream Christian doctrine, the full ins and outs of the intellectual history of the church, the modes of interaction with viewpoints from both inside and outside the church that offer alternatives to the main stream, and the principles of truth that must shape, critique, and re-shape the independent brainwork of our multi-cultural fallen world.

Regent College, where I have worked for over thirty years, has from the start labored to open the windows and point up the parameters for movement by evangelical students into the worlds of doctoral research and in due course of university faculty membership – the worlds, that is, of "Christianity-and" (or perhaps better, "Christianity-in"), where gospel truth may be brought to bear to leaven the lump of secular thought and endeavor. There is a border crossing here where my own heart has been anchored all along.

I would add that my journalistic work with the magazine *Christianity Today* has sought to express this same standpoint at a less technical level. I think of *CT* as called to be a centrist, unitive, life-embracing, and world-oriented publication that is educative, devotional, and culturally aware, having as its purpose the spiritual sensitizing and maturing of its readership in mainstream evangelical faith, in a ripened evangelical outlook, and in constant conscious submission to Abraham Kuyper's visionary dictum: "There is not a square inch in the whole domain of our human existence over which Christ, who is sovereign over all, does not cry: 'Mine!'" Augustinian, Calvinian, and Kuyperian are for me as an educator and communicator three names of honor of which I try to prove worthy in all that I do.

Serving Christ the King

It was Peter, preaching the gospel to Cornelius and

his household, who first celebrated Jesus Christ as "Lord of all" (Acts 10:36), and it was Paul who told the Colossians, and through them us, that in Him "are hidden all the treasures of wisdom and knowledge" (Colossians 2:3). It is not too much to say that those two texts have been, and still are, my ideological guiding stars. I have come to conceive the message of Christ in Chinese-box terms. The full significance of Christ's once-for-all atoning death for us will not be grasped till it is framed in our minds by the truth of Christ's triumphant resurrection and ascension, whereby the passage through death to eternal glory was opened for us; and the full significance of Christ's resurrection and ascension will not be grasped till we see it framed by the truth of Christ's omniscient and omnipotent presence here and now, with us and with all who honor and serve him, whoever and wherever we are in our passage through this world. Nor will the full significance of Christ's presence with us be appreciated until we recognize its global missional purpose. We cannot overemphasize the importance of the fact that Christ's promise, "I am with you always," was given within the context of global marching orders addressed to the church, as represented by the apostles – "Go. . . and make disciples of all nations" (Matthew 28:19-20).

The centrality of the *missio Dei* in the biblical revelation, and specifically in the New Testament, has in our time come to be appreciated at a deeper level than was the case before. The Latin phrase is a label for the movement of redemptive love whereby God acts in this world to further the goal of His own eternal glory and praise, from and through a covenant people remade in Christ. Jesus, Savior and Lord, the Son of God incarnate, is the focus and embodiment of the divine mission, the community of Christ's disciples is the agency through which the mission is carried on, and the church's missional task is two-pronged. One prong – or perhaps, for dignity's sake, I had better say project – is the extending and up-building of the church itself through evangelism, nurture and pastoral care; this, as we have seen, is where catechesis fits in as a necessary element in the strategy. The second prong, or project, is to model and propagate a re-angling and God-centrification, if I may coin a word, of the intellectual life and relational activity of all humankind: in other words, as Paul puts it, to "take every thought captive to obey Christ" (2 Corinthians 10:5).

For the whole world has now, by divine enactment, become the mediatorial kingdom of Christ (see, for instance, Luke 22:29-30; Colossians. 1:15; 1 Corinthians. 15:24-28), and in this kingdom the people of God armed with the gospel of God must ever be seeking to establish the authority of God by calling for recognition of, and submission to, the exalted Son of God, both by personal faith and by cultural endeavor. Neither our own world Christian community nor any that comes after us will ever be able to see this task as finished. God's people on earth will always find themselves called both to praise God for what has been accomplished and to attempt what has not been done yet. To adapt Eugene Peterson's haunting book title, the church's vocation will always be to an unending obedience in the same direction. So it will be till Christ returns.

The Higher Education Agenda

The business that brings us together at this time is what the world knows as higher education (tertiary education, in British parlance); that is, education at university and collegiate level in which the student's powers of critical judgment on evidence and on hypotheses and proposals based on evidence are being exercised and trained as part of the pedagogic discipline. It is in tertiary level teaching that I have earned my living for half a century, and what I wish to do in this closing section of my address is to reflect on how this common task of ours looks when set within the two-pronged missional frame that I have just described. If I may so phrase it, I want to unpack the Packer perspective on higher Christian education, so as to clarify as best I can what it is that I believe we are called to do.

The first thing to say is that in Christian higher education the catechetical viewpoint must always be maintained; in other words, the instructional procedure should constantly indicate, however briefly, how learners should live God-honoringly in light of the truth being taught. Colleges and universities are not churches, though there are certain obvious advantages in a situation where church and school operate as partners; but the fact remains that all truth is God's truth and requires appropriate forms of doxological response from all, so that in a Christian teaching institution explication of such response will very fittingly be part of the teaching syllabus, while syllabi that exclude this, for whatever reason, must be judged deficient by Christian standards. Evangelical and Roman Catholic colleges have in the past known this well, though today things are not always so clear – but that is another story.

I now move on to quote St. Paul. In the letter to the Colossians, having directed his readers' attention to "the riches of the glory of this mystery [long-hidden secret, now set forth in the gospel], which is Christ in you, the hope of glory," he continues:

Him we proclaim, warning everyone and
teaching everyone with all wisdom, that we
may present everyone mature in Christ . . .
I want you to know how great a struggle I
have for you . . . and for all who have not
seen me face to face, that their hearts may
be encouraged, being knit together in love,
to reach all the riches of full assurance of
understanding and the knowledge of God's
mystery, which is Christ, in whom are all
the treasures of wisdom and knowledge.
(Colossians 1:27-2:3)

Thus Paul conceived his task as an educator, and
we shall do well to take our cue, perspectivally, from him.
Implicit in his words I find four assumptions that together
yield the directional guidance we need for the fulfilling of
our share of the missional task.

First assumption: We humans, fundamentally,
are made in God's image; made to live rationally,
relationally, and responsibly; made to rule God's world
in righteousness as his representatives; and made to
respond to Him in joyful adoration and gratitude for
all the goodness that comes our way on a daily basis. As
Paul explains in such passages as Romans 1:18-3:18 and
Ephesians 2:1-3, 4:17-19, we have all lapsed ruinously from
that vocational ideal and are quite devoid of the wisdom
we need to relate to God; but assimilating the treasures of
wisdom found in Christ brings rediscovery of true, that is,
redeemed and re-centered, human life. Christian higher
education, comprehensively conceived and matched with
direct instruction in our churches, should be consciously
mediating that rediscovery all the time.

Second assumption: Truth is a unity, not only in

the simple sense that every true proposition is compatible
with every other, embodying as it does some element
of what God Himself knows, but also in the sense that
everything expresses diving sovereignty and connects
with Jesus Christ, who as the divine Son is co-creator and
upholder in being of everything (Colossians 1:16-17).
Thus the Son has a space-time involvement with literally
everything and everybody, being present and potent no
less where He is not acknowledged than where He is. Thus
He is the key to the unity of truth. This is part, at least, of
Paul's meaning when he speaks of treasures of wisdom
and knowledge hidden in Christ, and part, at least, of
the understanding of the world and its life that Christian
higher education must seek to promote.

    Third assumption: Knowledge has value; not
only the knowledge of spiritual things revealed via Christ,
which is what Paul speaks of here, but also the knowledge
of the created natural order and the providential course
of past history, each of which we rightly investigate by
the empirical scientific method of asking questions and
then going and looking for the answers. Knowledge
is for use, whether in personal fulfillment or in public
services or both. When, as recorded in Genesis 1:26,
God told Adam as mankind's representative to subdue
the earth, that meant getting to know our environment
and its possibilities so that we might manage it, harness
it, employ its resources wisely and put it to work as a
means to humankind's well-being. Paul speaks of the
value of spiritual knowledge as a path of spiritual life.
Christian higher education extends this principle, valuing
knowledge of created things and skills in harnessing
them as means for service in the family, the church, and
the community in personal, practical, technical, and
technological ways.

As therefore we have to work at shaping the curriculum in our colleges so that all facts appear in their Christian significance, ultimately as pointers to what the Bible classifies as godliness and good works, so we need to practice appropriate forms of fellowship in our colleges. This will surely mean that our faculty members will not, as in many teaching institutions, keep their distance from their students in order to husband time and energy for research. Rather, as elder brothers and sisters in the Christian college community, they will recognize an overall mentoring dimension to their calling, whereby they help students to see how to move ahead with the knowledge and formation that we are giving them.

Fourth assumption: Contemporary awareness must be maintained. Paul wrote Colossians to affirm the person and place of Jesus Christ in the context of a trendy distortion and aberration of which he was clearly well aware, having been thoroughly briefed on it, one imagines, by Epaphras, his Colossian informant. It is for us to affirm the significance of Christ in the context of the sad secularizing slippage of older Christian universities into an ultimate relativism, both intellectual and moral. The ideal of Christian education for which we stand is being left high and dry in the secular build-up of our self-styled post-Christian world, with its worship of technique, its vacuum of values, and its materialism and pessimism lurking just below the surface. We need to keep our eyes on this downward drift, unlovely as it is, and recognize that as the waves rise higher so our commitment to sustain the distinctives of Christian higher education must become ever clearer and stronger.

To indicate what this may mean, I close by citing two statements both taken from the promotional literature of Christian academic institutions (which, for what I hope are obvious reasons, I shall not identify). Together, it seems to me, they embody a thoroughly insightful and appropriately visionary response to the needs of our era in Christian higher education.

The first I clipped in 1996:

> A Christian college should be focused on the glory of God, rooted in reformed theology, nurturing disciples for Jesus Christ and leaders for the church, maintaining high standards of academic excellence while encountering culture apostolically and evangelistically, keeping faith with our own Christian heritage while rejoicing in and profiting from fellowship with other evangelicals.

The second, I clipped very recently:

> We will be a university that holds high God's word in all that we do and all that we are. We will be a university where we invite the Spirit of God to permeate our community in real ways and renewing ways. We will be a place where students matter to us because we see in them the future. So investing and loving and serving them will continue to be our hallmark. We will be a university where we strive for excellence in teaching and scholarship, known far and wide as a leader that champions biblical integration and intellectual vigor and rigor. We will be a university where mediocrity

is unacceptable and we will strive for the highest standards and professionalism in every degree program, department, school, building, performance, exhibit, competition, and publication. We will be a university that lovingly serves the world, courageously taking on the major challenges of our day where we are most suited to do so. We will be a university where students increasingly see in us the kind of higher education experience that they need to be prepared for meaningful careers and exemplary service for the cause of Christ.

It is my hope and prayer that God will make and keep all Christian higher educational institutions faithful to these guidelines.

References:

[1] Alister McGrath, *J. I. Packer: A Biography* (Grand Rapids: Baker Books, 1997), 280.

[2] Richard Baxter, *The Reformed Pastor* (1656; many editions).

Editor's note:

A signature of Tom's presidency was his devotion to students, and he was blessed by many reciprocating devotion to him. Of thousands of students whose lives were touched by Tom, perhaps Eric Motley was the one who developed the strongest and most lasting relationship. It began before Motley enrolled at Samford and maintained vitality to Tom's death. Motley is an extremely gifted intellectual, an eloquent speaker, a consummate Christian gentleman, a Samford graduate my brother respected greatly and loved like a son. Motley provides a moving personal tribute, epitomizing the feelings of many students who got to know my brother.

CHAPTER 11

A TRIBUTE TO MY PRESIDENT, MY MENTOR, MY FRIEND

By Eric L. Motley

I first met Dr. Thomas Corts during the summer
of 1991. I had been selected to represent Robert E. Lee
High School as the student representative at Alabama Boys
State, a summer leadership and citizenship program for
rising high school seniors, sponsored by The American
Legion and The American Legion Auxiliary. For one
week in July, I joined more than 300 young men from
across Alabama on Samford University's beautiful campus.
Walking from building to building, I came to think of the
place as everything I ever imagined a university to look
like – rolling hills, spires, cupolas, columns, bell towers,
uniform red-brick, colonial-style buildings, and great gates
at the front entrance. The excitement I felt awakened
something deep within – a serious awareness and an

appreciation for my own personal aspirations and, like never before, a desire to attend university.

Two events that week impacted my life. The first was being elected governor. A mock election with a full slate of state officials and representatives to the state legislature, including governor and cabinet positions, is one of the highpoints of Boys State. After delivering a speech on the need to support better education, I was urged to run for governor. I campaigned hard, shook many hands, made many promises, and in the end won the election. In essence, I became Alabama's first black governor! The win earned me a trip to Boys Nation in Washington, D.C.

The second was listening to a speech delivered by Samford's president, Dr. Thomas Corts. His message urged us to live out a great, God-directed destiny, stating that Alabama needed us as young men to lead and bring principled leadership to the issues of our time. His words struck a nerve deep inside, and as I sat listening to him in the great concert hall of Samford, I began to think how I could possibly attend this wonderful institution. More generally, I began to ponder the way in which I could personally achieve some of the goals and aspirations he encouraged us all to pursue.

Returning home to my small town of Madison Park near Montgomery, Alabama, my grandparents (essentially my parents because they raised me from birth) encouraged me to follow my dream, but we all knew it would take a herculean effort. Mrs. Watterson, my twelfth grade English teacher, proved to be the turning point. As she coached me on writing my college essays, Mrs. Watterson discovered my longing to attend Samford. She immediately went into action, sending word through her husband, a friend of Dr. Corts, and declaring, "If you do not enroll this young man, Samford will miss one of the two or three finest students I have ever taught." Somehow scholarship money and money for extras was found, provided by many friends and family in and around Montgomery. As a result I found myself enrolled at Samford University.

From the beginning, I jumped in with eager enthusiasm. At age nineteen, my dream of attending Samford had come true, and I wanted to take advantage of every opportunity I could to learn and develop. As president of my freshman class and an active participant in student government, I never met a stranger. Typically up for a jog at 4:30 or 5:00 a.m. I quickly got to know everyone on campus, from students, parents, and professors to maintenance and sanitation workers and everyone in between.

But there was no one I wanted to get to know more than Dr. Corts. He intrigued me – his grace, humility, and intellectual curiosity, his commitment to knowledge and to Christ. Even though I did not know him well, I could tell he was a remarkable example of faith and leadership. I began to seek him out. If I saw him on campus, I would disengage myself from friends to walk across and engage him in even a few minutes of conversation. I was like a painter, studying his subject. I wanted to get to know the very essence of this man, to hold him up to the light and find the watermark. I was not afraid to take the initiative by writing him notes and dropping them off - that is how I got to know all the secretaries.

Dr. Corts was the university president, but somehow, increasingly over time, we became friends. Not in public places or under the spotlight so that others could see, but gradually he became my personal teacher, my example, my mentor, editing out all of the excesses of my life, helping me to appreciate the nuances and subtleties of language and the profundity of silence. He recognized my deep longing to grow and develop, and he nurtured that desire by sending me handpicked articles and magazines. He took the time to teach me about the incremental – how day by day, week by week, year by year, the small decisions add up to the great consequences, and ultimately add up to life. He shared with me the thoughts that captivated him when his mind and heart were young and tender, all with the hope that I might see them the same way and discover for myself the wonders of nature just as he had. What he said, how he said it, how he lived it, I recorded it, letting it make an indelible impression in my mind and heart.

During my junior year at Samford, Dr. Corts shared his vision for the future of Samford, and I was quite taken with it. As vice president of the student government association, I decided similarly to create a strategic program for continuing quality improvement on campus. To do this, I organized 6:00 a.m. breakfast meetings with student leaders, brought in speakers and thought leaders – anyone I could find who might help us develop a workable strategy. Then I took our plan to Dr. Corts. Incredibly, he took the time to go through it and thoughtfully help me understand that it was good, but not good enough. He took me seriously, and he took our plan seriously. I will never forget that.

When I look back I cannot help but to appreciate how rich and magical my days were at Samford. I discovered myself anew, and Dr. Corts was the most influential person in my life. Since then, I have had the privilege of being around many highly intelligent, impressive people. Dr. Corts still remains at the top of the list. I have still not met a person that I have desired to be more like, to emulate more in body, spirit, and soul, than Dr. Corts. Men and women included, I have never met a more Christ-like person than he, and yet, Dr. Corts never spoke much about his spiritual intimacies, not publicly. Often as Christians we want to talk about God and our faith. He did not. The old adage, "Preach the gospel and use words when necessary," was Dr. Corts. He was a man who lived his faith, and that meant the world to a young man trying to come to grips with his spiritual life and the direction of his future. I wanted to know God like he knew Him. I wanted to experience that enlightenment. I knew the more time I could spend with Dr. Corts, the more polished I could become.

Over the seventeen years of our relationship, I came to appreciate that there were very few individuals like Dr. Corts. He was rare and one-of-kind, inasmuch as one can be one-of-kind. His articulation of what was right and noble, his sense of faith and civitas, his profound understanding of the vitality of education in society, not for some or those who could afford it, but for all, was the sure foundation that all else was built upon.

It is true, time allows us growth and understanding, and it also allows us to re-adjust our admiration and estimation of those we have idolized. The more we learn of them, the more access we have to their inward thinking and personal motivations, all the more ordinary they often become to us. But on the contrary, the more I was exposed to the man, Dr. Corts, the more I examined his thoughts and delved into the personal chambers of his life and his way of living, the more I came to appreciate the smooth consistency of his living, the integrity of his person, the clarity of his thinking, the purity of his intellectual pursuits, the gravity of his capacity to be concerned and to love others, and the more I grew to admire him.

After I left Samford, we continued to stay in touch. My grandfather died while I was in Scotland working on my masters and doctorate, and Dr. Corts was the second person I called after learning the news. Later, after I moved to Washington and was serving as special assistant to President Bush, I had an opportunity to do a photo shoot with the president. My grandmother could not come, so my boss agreed to let me bring in Dr. Corts and several other individuals who had made my education possible. I look at that photo, sitting on my office credenza, every day. After he moved to Washington to fulfill his position with the U.S. AID program, Dr. Corts and I often met for dinner after work. There was never a big decision that I did not discuss first with Dr. Corts.

To this day I carry a letter from him in my briefcase and a printout of the last email he sent me, just three days before his untimely passing.

> Many thanks, again, Eric, for my book. As I have been home and had opportunity, I have been re-reviewing my books and your fingerprints are on many of them, for which I am grateful. They inspire me to think of many joyous experiences, both here and abroad in Scotland and England.
>
> REMember: it's all about R-E-M – relationships, experiences, memories."

Yes, Dr. Corts, I will remember. My goal at Samford was to discover the deepest essence of your being. Graciously, you shared your Christian mind, your Christian walk, the beauty and promise you saw in all things, your good taste and appreciation for quality, your wise interpretation of the everyday matters of life. You were the fulfillment of your own belief that every gift is an offering to God and only the best should be rendered. You have been and will continue to be, my inspiration for living both the life of the mind and the Christian life. In my remembrance of you I am filled with *Gratitude.*

Editor's Note:

Though Tom would have protested the title and the high praise within this essay, Roger Lovette writes from a highly personal vantage point spanning over forty years. He knew my brother for so many years, in so many different roles, in so many different relationships, through so many different experiences, and in so many varied public and private settings. Roger's epideictic oratory, recorded here as essay, reflects one person's candid perspective, and anecdotally he portrays Tom as a man who thought and lived Christianly. As a preacher and writer, Roger is gifted with a unique art of expression well displayed in this essay.

CHAPTER 12

GREAT TOM

By Roger Lovette

T.S. Matthews once wrote a biography of the poet,
T.S. Eliot. It was an unusual biography because it was not
overly academic. The book dealt with the poetic journey
into the creative soul of a fellow human being and was
entitled, *Great Tom*. When I think of Tom Corts I cannot
help but remember that title because it fits Tom Corts to
a tee – Great Tom. And being once his pastor and a long-
time friend I do not have the credentials to talk about his
academic achievements, which were many, but I can talk
about the poetry of his life. I knew this best.

Of course, he would have protested this title: Great
Tom. And being the word-master he was, Tom would, in
his inimitable way challenge my use of the word *great*. And
in defense, I would say this word means many things:

Impressive . . .
    Imposing . . .
        Important . . .
            Lofty . . .
                Profound.
He was shy when such a spotlight would shine on
him. He would say that none of these words applied to
him. And reluctantly in my disagreement I would tell him
he was wrong.

Why Great Tom?

I saw Tom up close in a multitude of settings
through the years. Our paths first crossed when he was
chair of the search committee of Faith Baptist Church in
Georgetown, Kentucky. The year was 1969, and we met
one cold January day. Tom was twenty-eight years old and
already assistant to the president of Georgetown College.
Even though I did not know much about him, I knew even
then that this young man was someone special.

I met his wife Marla and their children that
weekend. I still remember little Rachel sitting on their
kitchen island in an infant seat. Jennifer, just a little older,
played on the floor. Little did I realize that weekend would
be the beginning of a very special friendship.

I was his pastor for six years. I watched him be a
good husband and attentive father. I watched him mow
his little yard with an old-fashioned push-mower. When I
would ask him why in the world he did not get a gasoline
mower he just looked at me with that certain Tom Corts
look. "It's good exercise," he said.

The little church in Georgetown was made up
primarily of college professors and students. Most of us

lived on a shoestring, but we squeezed all the fun and joy we could out of those six years. He was a good churchman and fought fiercely for his pastor and his church. Tom helped enormously when we built an addition to our building with very little money. He was chair of the building committee. We had a member who was in the construction business, and Tom picked his brain and put this man on our building committee. He saw gifts in this man that could easily have been overlooked. We could not have built that building without that man's tireless help. On Dedication Day, Tom stood in front of all those academics and reminded us that this quiet man with no college ties had helped us do what none of us could have done without him. Tom brought this member whom few knew into the circle, and the church became larger that day. I would see him do this again and again through the years.

Tom discovered those of us who had birthdays and anniversaries around the same time, and he planned events in Georgetown, Frankfort, and Louisville to celebrate each other's special moments. Even then I recognized that Tom loved good food, nice surroundings, and things done well. It would be a quality that would take him all the way to the finish line. We had a hard time wrenching the check away from Tom. He always wanted to pay; he was generous to a fault.

During those years Tom was working on his doctorate in rhetoric at Indiana University. How he balanced job and family and long drives to Bloomington must have been difficult. What a hard worker he was. When he moved to Birmingham in 1983 to be president of Samford University he asked me to come and take part in a prayer service on the day of his installation. None of us who gathered there knew what the future would hold, but we did know that whatever took place under his leadership would be good and fine and rich and rare. We were not wrong.

He flew to Clemson and Memphis when I was installed in the churches there. When I moved back to Birmingham in 1993 Tom was part of that installation service in my new church. He always had time to reach out and help a friend.

His accomplishments at Samford were multitudinous; I will leave that long distinguished list to someone else. However, one of the wonderful things he did was to establish the London Centre, hoping that students would learn to love England as he did and find their Alabama world stretched and stretched. Hundreds of students have participated in that program.

At his funeral I remembered something that was said of Sir Christopher Wren, one of the great English architects. Wren designed St. Paul's in London and a multitude of other famous buildings, and the preacher remarked at his funeral, "If you would see his monuments, look around you." I asked those gathered at Tom's funeral to look around them. The Wright Fine Arts Center on Samford's campus was packed with a multitude of people: governors, senators, leaders in the community, teachers, administrators, domestics, and students, students everywhere.

When I retired from my Birmingham Church in 2000, Tom, who had been in my life since 1969, was still there. He prayed a beautiful prayer at my retirement service. Those who knew him knew he had a wonderful way with words, and that prayer was moving and breathtaking. This is part of what he prayed:

We offer thanks for his ministry in multiple places,
Among the churches that nurtured him,
tolerated him, encouraged him,
Among the well-known and the unknown,
Among those who celebrate here today,
Among those who cannot even
remember his name . . .
But remember Yours because
of him. "

I think of his words as I write this tribute. For in the years to come students will walk across Samford's campus and Wingate's campus and Georgetown's campus and even though they may not have known Tom Corts personally, they will know the Father's name because of what Tom did while he served so faithfully.

His leave-taking was sudden and painful for us all, but not as heartbreaking as it has been for dear Marla and Jennifer and Rachel and Chris. Just two evenings before his death, he was so proud to hear that Chris and his wife were expecting. It turned out they had twins and one of those babies was named for their grandfather, Thomas Edward Corts. This family will always have what this good and kind man gave them year after year.

Tom loved quotes. Years before in Kentucky he had given me a particular phrase I found most meaningful. On the day of his funeral I gave those words back to him. They came from Fyodor Dostoevsky's *The Brothers Karamazov.* "And even if we are occupied with important things, even if we attain honor or fall into misfortune, still let us remember how good it was once here when we were all together, united by a good and kind feeling which made us better perhaps than we are."

Great Tom – how he blessed so many of us. But as I think about his legacy I think of the personal times: the business meetings when he pled for raises for his pastor, the candle-lit dinners in fine restaurants when we wrestled him for the check, the gifts he always brought on special occasions in our lives, the fierce determination he brought to every task and, most of all, his opening up of his heart and letting so many of us in.

Tom Corts – Great Tom.

> Impressive . . .
> Imposing . . .
> Important . . .
> Lofty . . .
> Profound.

But more than these – a man of faith and hope and love.

Editor's Note:

Bill Nunnelley was serving in Samford's University Relations Department when Tom became Samford's president in 1983 and served there throughout Tom's tenure of service. When Samford President Andrew Westmoreland and I were discussing this memorial book project, Westmoreland immediately spoke up as we talked about someone to write a brief biography of Tom, saying there would not be anyone better to do that than Bill Nunnelley. Nunnelley continues on the Samford staff with more than thirty years of service.

CHAPTER 13

A LIFE OF STUDY, SERVICE, AND CHRISTIAN DEDICATION: A SHORT BIOGRAPHY OF THOMAS E. CORTS

By William A. Nunnelley

Born in Terre Haute, Indiana, on October 7, 1941, Thomas E. Corts grew up in Ashtabula, Ohio, one of seven siblings. A pastor in the local Christian church, his father Charles combined ministry with ownership of a proprietary business school. Money did not come easily for the nine-member Corts family. Even though parents and siblings worked hard, there never seemed to be an extra nickel. Growing up in the 1940s and 50s, Tom learned early on what it took to earn a dollar – a lesson he never forgot. "I was always amazed at how my parents could stretch a dollar," he recalled in 2006. As a youngster Tom washed cars for a funeral home, delivered newspapers, and clerked at a corner store, sometimes netting as much as $9 a week, a sizable sum for that day and time.

Young Tom balanced work with a voracious appetite for reading and his family's church activities. He was so involved with church that high school classmates nicknamed him "Reverend." Unlike his older brothers, however, Tom did not dream of a career in the pulpit. Instead, he pursued journalism and worked for the local newspaper, covering Friday night football games. Never did he guess that one day he would be responsible for managing entire college athletic programs.

Though Tom would choose a different career path, his youthful involvement with church and its values directed him toward a lifelong pursuit of ministry and service. In fact, the traits of scholarship and Christian study would lay the foundation for his entire adult life.

College Life and Early Career

Following graduation from Ashtabula High School, young Tom headed off to college. After one year at Trinity Bible College in Clearwater, Florida, he switched to Georgetown College in Kentucky, where he completed his undergraduate degree in 1963. There, Corts caught the attention of Georgetown president Dr. Robert Mills, who recognized the young man's leadership ability.

Taking an interest, Mills asked Corts to serve as his assistant for one year, post graduation. Discovering a natural affinity for the inner workings of higher education, Tom began to see how he might combine his faith, love of education, and his family's tradition of service. "I always thought my life should be dedicated to the Lord," Corts recalled. "That year at Georgetown was a life-changing experience. I loved working with the college. It just seemed to me that it was a rich and full way to live your life – to work with the church, to work with young people, to talk books and intellectual ideas. That was very appealing to me."

During that year at Georgetown, Tom married his high school sweetheart, Marla Haas, who had recently graduated from Houghton College in New York. The couple would eventually round out their family with two daughters, Jennifer and Rachel, and one son, Christian.

After completing a master's degree and a doctorate at Indiana University, Corts returned to Georgetown College, serving as director of planning and development, executive dean, and finally executive vice president. "He was clearly very gifted even at that early age," recalled fellow faculty member Dr. Joe Lewis. Corts also served a year as coordinator of the Higher Education Consortium of Kentucky. Then, at the age of thirty-two, with a wealth of administrative experience behind him, Corts became president of Wingate College, a two-year Baptist school near Charlotte, North Carolina, in 1974.

Corts would spend the next nine years at Wingate. Realizing that the school would face a brighter future as a four-year institution, he led Wingate to add upper level courses and majors. The school granted its first baccalaureate degrees in 1979. A staunch believer in the value of international education in a global society, Corts also instituted an international program known as W'International, in which every student could spend ten days abroad during their sophomore year. "W'International was a very novel idea that garnered national attention for the school," recalled wife Marla.

Transition to Samford University

During the summer and fall of 1982, Samford University began actively pursuing a successor to its longtime president, Dr. Leslie Wright, who planned to retire in 1983. Eventually, Samford's search committee identified Corts as the best candidate to succeed Wright. Corts had no thoughts of leaving. He and Marla had just built a new home for their family and were prepared to stay at Wingate a long time. But Samford's trustees were insistent, and their persuasive powers proved successful, especially those of board members A. Gerow Hodges and Harry B. Brock, Jr., who spent long hours introducing Corts to the Birmingham community and explaining why a move to Samford would be in Corts's best interest.

According to the late Dr. Hudson Baggett, then editor of *The Alabama Baptist* newspaper, Corts "blew the group out of the water" during one of his visits to Birmingham to meet with Samford's presidential search committee. Baggett told Jack Brymer, his associate editor, "Tom Corts will be the next president of Samford University." On September 1, 1983, Dr. Thomas E. Corts officially assumed the post that would become the defining position of his career.

Dawn of a New Era

On a blue-sky autumn day in November 1983, with colorful banners representing Samford's seven colleges fluttering in the breeze, an academic procession of several hundred educators and associates walked across campus to the Wright Center for the inauguration of Thomas Edward Corts, the university's seventeenth president. Twelve-year old Christian Corts held a Bible as his father took the oath of office. Board of Trustees chairman Ben B. Brown placed the presidential medallion around the neck of Samford's new leader.

A New Era Dawns – That simple phrase, illustrated with a rising sun, adorned various printed pieces and mementoes and heralded Corts's launch of a new administration. In his inaugural address, Corts explained that he brought no "satchel full of tricks, a grand plan, something to be unfolded, readily announced, soon implemented" that would vault the school into some higher level of accomplishment or status. Rather, he promised hard work and a team effort that would make Samford "even better." He added, "The best has not been, it is yet to be, and that is the finest tribute we can make to all of those who have been part of the illustrious past of this place."

The new president set about to make good his promise of "even better." What would become one of his brightest accomplishments occurred in his first year – the purchase of a Samford study center in the heart of London, England. Emphasizing once again his belief in the value of international education, Tom led the purchase of a former bed-and-breakfast hotel in the Kensington-Chelsea borough of the British capital that could be used year-round by Samford students. This purchase formed the focal point of an international program that would eventually expand and touch five continents. In 1984, the first group of students spent the fall semester in London. Since then, more than 10,000 students and faculty have used the twenty-six-room facility now known as Daniel House.

Corts also brought back intercollegiate football, dormant for ten years, in an effort to boost school spirit and enrollment. He emphasized the announcement by firing a perfect spiral pass to a university colleague at the end of a press conference announcing the new sport, as a roomful of cameras snapped and whirred.

The next few years brought a succession of noteworthy additions – computer intensification, the first residence hall construction in twenty-five years, a nursing school building. In 1988, with the help of former Alabama Governor Albert Brewer, Samford established the Public Affairs Research Council of Alabama, the state's first nonpartisan fact-finding body for public policy. The same year, Samford opened the first divinity school, Beeson Divinity School, on the campus of a Southern Baptist university. "It's the Lord's money . . . and I'm going to give it back to Him," explained Ralph W. Beeson, whose gift funded the new school. Two years later, Beeson died, leaving Samford an estate gift that ultimately reached $54.8 million, the largest in Alabama history.

As Samford approached its 150ᵗʰ anniversary, Corts determined to make the event a high profile celebration. Chartered by Alabama Baptists in late 1841 and opened in early 1842, Samford followed suit, spanning its sesquicentennial celebration over eighteen months in 1991 and 1992. Corts invited former British Prime Minister Margaret Thatcher to cap off the festivities. Visiting on April 7, 1992, Thatcher insisted on a campus walk-around to greet students before delivering an address on international affairs later that night. "Always stay strong or you won't be able to stop the tyrant in the future," she advised in her speech.

In 1994, Samford trustees voted to change the university charter to elect its own members. The body stressed its commitment to Baptist and Christian principles, and the university worked hard to keep the support of the Alabama Baptist State Convention. In the Winter 1994 issue of Samford's magazine, *Seasons*, Corts defined that commitment.

> To be a Baptist university is to be a Christian university. It is important for us to acknowledge that Baptists began Howard College (Samford's name prior to 1965) and have sustained it over the years with direct denominational gifts, as well as with prayers, encouragement, and goodwill of congregations and individuals. We have a strong identity with Alabama Baptists, with Baptists world-wide, and with the wider Christian community. We see our Christian emphasis as distinctive, making Samford different from state-supported institutions, which by law and precedent have to be cautious about religion. We require courses in Bible and participation in convocation. We encourage dealing with spiritual, moral, and ethical issues in classes and in extracurricular activities. We provide ministry experiences for our students and seek to nurture students' personal faith. This is a community of faith and learning, as the motto 'Deo et Doctrinae' attests, and we value higher standards of personal responsibility, as a result.

In the 1980s, *U.S. News & World Report* began publishing its best colleges in the nation feature. Corts pondered how Samford might gain the magazine's attention. While some schools hired public relations firms to get noticed, he decided to do the opposite. "Let's just go about being a good university and see if anybody notices," he was quoted as saying. So Samford chipped away with what Corts described as "a lot of hard, day-to-day, year-to-year work by a lot of people."

The approach worked. In 1989, the magazine chose Samford as an "up-and-coming" university. The following year, 1990, it recognized Samford as one of the best schools in the South, and it remains on the list today. "The ranking has been hugely important to our continuing to enroll outstanding students, and to become branded as a university serious about academics and serious about its Christian commitment," Corts stated in 2006.

Leading a Constitutional Reform

Corts was proud of Samford and eager to share its message wherever he could. One day in 1999, he spoke to the Birmingham Kiwanis Club. But this time, the message was different. "People went thinking they were going to hear a speech about Samford," recalled Albert Brewer, "but they came away knowing a great deal more about the need for constitutional reform in the state. And he carried that message all over Alabama." Brewer credited the speech with starting Alabama's constitutional reform movement.

In his Kiwanis speech, Corts explained that Alabama had "such great capacity, so many positive attributes," that he tired of seeing its consistent low ranking in national studies. He blamed such results on Alabama's constitution, a document "bloated with excess specificity" that left concentrating power in the hands of the state legislature. He called for a constitutional convention to rewrite the 1901 document, the nation's longest with more than 220,000 words and 661 amendments. Because it stipulated what government could not do, constitutional change could only be made in the form of amendments.

As founding chairman of the Alabama Citizens for

Constitutional Reform, Corts led the charge to revise the obsolete document, this in addition to being president of a private university that received no state funds. One civic leader pointedly asked about Corts's involvement, saying, "Samford's dog is not in that hunt, is it?" Corts offered a polite answer. "Our first obligation is to serve the public as a university," he said.

Retired former Samford provost William E. Hull said later that such a stance was typical of the Samford president. "Corts was unafraid to challenge the status quo because his conscience was not captive to the latest poll." Shortly before his retirement, Corts reiterated his belief in the effort. "I want to see the Alabama Constitution reformed, and I'll do anything I can for that cause," he told interviewer Jack Brymer. Despite Corts's efforts, and those of numerous other like-minded citizens, Alabama still operates under its 1901 constitution, which now has almost 1,000 amendments.

Growing the Endowment

During the 1950s, '60s and '70s, Samford invested heavily in building its Lakeshore Drive campus. When Corts arrived as president in 1983, the school's endowment stood at a modest $8 million. The Board of Trustees charged the new president with growing that figure. An aggressive investment program coupled with generous gifts spurred the college's most dramatic period of growth. In 2006, despite the economic downturns in the 2000s, the figure stood at more than $250 million.

During the mid-1990s, under Corts's leadership, Samford's campus grew rapidly with the construction of Divinity Hall and Chapel (now Andrew Gerow Hodges

Chapel), Lucille Stewart Beeson Law Library and a major addition to the Harwell G. Davis Library known as Hudnall Library. Former President Gerald R. Ford spoke at the law library dedication. In 2000, the U.S. Secretary of Education, Richard Riley, presented the first National Award for Effective Teacher Preparation to Samford's Orlean Bullard Beeson School of Education and Professional Studies. In 2001 Samford completed its largest academic building, a $29 million science center now named William R. Propst Hall.

Corts described those years of intensive development as "great fun," adding, "You'd like to think that, long term, they are going to be seen as great advantages." Asked what the most challenging aspect of his role as president was, he quickly answered, "Finding money! . . . Finding discretionary funds to do the things that great institutions ought to be doing." During Corts's tenure, more than $207 million in capital projects were accomplished. None of the monies came from the operating budget. "When I look back, I'm extremely glad we did them," Corts stated. "If we were to start them now, they would cost so much more."

Outside Leadership Endeavors

The quintessential educator, Corts served as chairman of the Commission on Colleges of the Southern Association of Colleges and Schools (SACS) and later as president of SACS, the accrediting agency for universities and colleges in eleven southern states. As SACS president, he led a major revision of the organization's self-study guidelines. He also served as president of the American Association of Presidents of Independent Colleges and

Universities and of the National Fellowship of Baptist Educators. In 2006, President George W. Bush appointed Corts to the J. William Fulbright Foreign Scholarship Board.

Post Samford: Pursuing the "the Vita Contemplativa"

Corts announced in April 2005 his intention to retire at the conclusion of the 2006 spring semester. Speaking to a called meeting of faculty and staff members in Reid Chapel, he said, "Life requires a lot of twists and turns. Growing up in the Midwest, never did I ask, 'Lord, get me to Alabama as fast as you can. Never did I expect to become a full-fledged Alabamian – but here I stand." He considered himself "a very blessed man, because I have been privileged to do what I wanted to do, and what I felt was the work given me to do, and what is more, I have enjoyed it!" It had been a life of action, he acknowledged.

What would he now do? Pursue "the vita contemplativa," the life of contemplation, Corts explained in his retirement announcement. Speaking to his final commencement on May 20, 2006, the outgoing president stressed the importance of authenticity to the 832 graduating seniors. Then, just as he had done with every graduation ceremony in his tenure, Corts awarded each senior a hand-signed diploma. In all, Corts distributed more than 18,000 hand-signed diplomas during his twenty-three years as president.

But his life of contemplation was not to be. No sooner had he stepped down as Samford president than Alabama Governor Bob Riley asked him to serve as interim chancellor of the troubled Alabama College System of twenty-six two-year schools – the toughest assignment of his career. "I would consider accepting this responsibility a fulfillment of a sense of civic duty, and I would do it out of a desire to help," he said. Corts stepped into a system embroiled in a joint federal and state investigation involving allegations of corruption and nepotism. Governor Riley appointed Corts in an effort to provide stable leadership while the state board of education sought a permanent chancellor. "Education is a noble calling," Corts said, "and this kind of thing (the practices under investigation) should not go on." During his seven months as interim chancellor, Corts succeeded in pointing the beleaguered program in the right direction. Investigations ferreted out some of the system's chief offenders and convictions soon followed.

In the fall of 2007, after Corts had accepted a post as executive director of the International Association of Baptist Colleges and Universities, President Bush called on him to serve as coordinator of The President's Initiative to Expand Education, and subsequently, as coordinator of Basic Education in the Office of the Director of Foreign Assistance. The State Department-based program provided aid to four million children in six underserved nations: Ethiopia, Ghana, Honduras, Liberia, Mali, and Yemen. It would be Corts's final assignment.

Writer, Researcher, Student, Scholar

Corts was an accomplished communicator with a talent for crafting and delivering a moving speech, or creating an incisive work of prose. "I've always been fascinated by the spoken word . . . what [words] mean, how you can stream them together to reach certain ends," he said in a 2006 interview. Some of this grew out of his involvement in an early debate course and a classically oriented instructor who introduced him to Greek and Roman theories of rhetoric. Another influence, he told a colleague, was an editor he encountered while working part-time at *The Clearwater Sun* in Florida who encouraged him to "always look for the two-fisted quote."

Corts also demonstrated an unusual devotion to research. When delving into a topic, "he wanted to make sure that the information he had was complete," recalled Samford archivist Elizabeth C. Wells, who worked with Corts on numerous research projects over the years. Corts loved the integrity of facts and made good use of them.

"When he wrote a speech, a column, gave a speech or comment, he was prepared and told the 'story' honestly," Wells described. Corts frequently called on Wells to assist in researching a question or issue. "The time frame could be two to three hours, maybe a day, but once it was fifteen minutes!" she said.

Wells recalled Corts's meticulous work on the book, *Bliss and Tragedy: The Ashtabula Railway-Bridge Accident of 1876 and the Loss of P. P. Bliss*, which he edited. "He did his own research, reading month after month, page after page of the Ashtabula newspaper on microfilm," she said. The book detailed the accident, which killed ninety-two people in Corts's hometown and is still regarded as the nation's worst railroad disaster of the nineteenth century. Corts himself wrote the chapter on Bliss, the composer of such well-known hymns as "Hold the Fort," "Almost Persuaded," and "It Is Well with My Soul." Corts also spent untold hours in the Library of Congress researching the life of Horatio Spafford, author of the words to "It Is Well with My Soul." Corts's manuscript on Spafford was published following his death.

As a student of debate and classical rhetoric, Corts

developed an appreciation for effective communicators and well-written passages. He claimed no favorite orator, but admitted a fascination for William Jennings Bryan, the three-time Democratic presidential candidate and secretary of state under President Woodrow Wilson. "I've always admired Bryan's Christian perspective," he said. "He was one of the few people who was very strong in his Christianity but quite liberal in his politics." Corts noted that Bryan "was hated by Wall Street manipulators," adding, "his reputation has been unfairly damaged by the success of the play, *Inherit the Wind*, which is certainly not historically accurate." As for strong writing, Corts described Lincoln's Gettysburg Address as "a phenomenal piece of word craft." Lincoln "must have mulled over some of those phrases, even though the entire speech was written in a fairly short time," he said.

Corts's love for words extended quite naturally into the world of books. He loved reading biography and non-fiction. "I read some fiction," he admitted once, "but rarely." One of his favorite books was Henry Drummond's *The Greatest Thing in the World*, which he described as "timeless."

At the age of fourteen, Corts began a lifelong pursuit of buying books and building a personal library. He loved browsing in old bookstores, looking for treasures that he might add to his and Marla's voluminous collection. This was especially true of their periodic visits to England and Samford's London study centre. They explored bookstores in every British city and town they visited, invariably returning with shopping bags filled with books. "We crated up boxes to be shipped home," Marla recalled.

Corts had a special appreciation for rare volumes with fore-edge paintings. He described such books in a *Seasons* column, noting that he was thirty-two before he saw his first one. "Fore-edge paintings are elaborate illustrations painted, not in a book, or on the cover or spine, but on the edges of the pages," he wrote. The individual pages reveal little of the painting, and the scene becomes visible "only when knowledgeable hands compress the pages at the proper angle." Corts likened the technique to the manner in which Samford students, "each lending a story, a uniqueness to the Samford composite," together reveal a "delightful picture of a vital university."

Corts also possessed "an ongoing sense of being an archivist," recalled Marla, particularly where family history was concerned. "Tom held a sense of how things should endure and was very intentional in his keeping of records about family vacations and such," she said. Over the years Corts meticulously kept daily journals and would often read from them on family occasions. "Our kids loved that," she said.

Corts always maintained a strong sense of family commitment. "He had such loyalty to his siblings and would move heaven and earth to try to help them," Marla said. Tom initiated annual family heritage tours to Indiana and Ohio, Marla said, visiting sites that were a part of family lore. "We would start in Star City, Indiana, where Tom's father first joined a church and where his parents are buried, and work our way back to Ashtabula. We would always go past his father's old church. On one trip we discovered the lot was vacant. The church had been torn down. Tom searched the area for a local historian and finally found a man who knew about the church. About all that was left were two pews. Tom had one crated up and sent to our home. We also salvaged a stained glass window. I marveled at his energy for that kind of thing," Marla recalled.

The Summation of a Life Well Lived

Growing up in a Christian family, Corts said he "always felt that whatever I did ought to be a ministry." At the age of ten or twelve, he enjoyed listening to extended family theological debates. "I can't ever remember a time when I did not in my heart want to be a Christian," he said. "When I was fourteen or fifteen, I bought a *Cruden's Concordance* because I was having trouble finding references in the Bible. That was one of the earliest books I acquired."

Even so, Corts did not choose the same path as his siblings. "We all had the sense that the Lord had high expectations of us," said Corts, though his three older brothers became ministers while Corts found his calling in education. "I've always thought that the work I did here at Samford is something of a ministry . . . I do view it as a ministry," he said. At a retirement dinner in the spring of 2006, Corts responded to some tributes to him by quoting Thomas Carlyle, who said, "Blessed is he who has found his work. He needs no other blessedness."

Corts also recalled a prophetic statement from his friend, Jarvis Warren, in 1983. As he contemplated moving to Samford from Wingate, "Jarvis told me, 'At age forty-one, if you go to Samford, you are going to give them the best years of your life.' He was right. I have, and I have no regrets."

Corts's life was cut short by a heart attack February 4, 2009. Just sixteen days earlier he had completed his presidential appointment with the State Department. He was sixty-seven years old.

When he announced his impending retirement from Samford in 2005, Corts said he looked forward to a life of contemplation. But as a man devoted to service, he instead found his "vita contemplative" by continuing to serve through leadership positions that furthered his vision of better education on all levels, both private and public. This only underscored what he said to *Seasons* magazine in the spring of 2006, "I do not want to be on a shelf."

Corts did not live his life on a shelf, but served with his whole heart, mind, and body until the very day God called him home.

ABOUT THE CONTRIBUTORS

Paul R. Corts (Editor) was born the sixth of seven children to Charles and Hazel Corts and is the younger brother of Tom Corts. Paul currently serves as president of the Council for Christian Colleges & Universities in Washington, D.C. From 2002 to 2006, he served as Assistant Attorney General for Administration in the U. S. Department of Justice. Prior to that, Corts held presidencies at Palm Beach Atlantic University and Wingate College and faculty and administrative positions at Oklahoma Baptist University and Western Kentucky University. Corts has served in leadership roles in many professional organizations and is the author of two college textbooks and several publications, including his most recent work, *Caring for the President.* Corts holds a bachelor's degree from Georgetown College and master's and doctoral degrees from Indiana University. He and his wife, Diane, are the parents of three grown children.

John Robert Walmsley Stott (1921 - 2011) was born in London and served as rector of All Souls Church, Langham Place, London, from 1950 to 1975. A noted leader of the worldwide Evangelical movement, *TIME* magazine ranked Stott among the 100 most influential people in the world in 2005. During the International Congress on World Evangelization in Lausanne, Switzerland, 1974, Stott served as the chairman of the Drafting Committee for the Lausanne Covenant. He founded the London Institute for Contemporary Christianity in 1982 and Langham Partnership International, a ministry with influence in more than 100 countries. The author of more than fifty books, Stott's best-known works include *Basic Christianity, The Cross of Christ, Understanding the Bible, The Contemporary Christian, Christ the Controversialist, The Epistles of John* (Tyndale Commentary), *Evangelical Truth, Issues Facing Christians Today, Christian Mission in the Modern World, The Incomparable Christ,* and *Why I Am a Christian.* Stott passed away in London on July 27, 2011. He was ninety years old.

William E. Hull is a research professor at Samford University in Birmingham, Alabama, where he also served as provost and Theologian in Residence at Mountain Brook Baptist Church in Birmingham. He is a distinguished educator, minister, and author of several books, including *Strategic Preaching, Harbingers of Hope,* and *Seminary in Crisis.* Thomas Corts called Hull "one of the most analytical, synthesizing, eclectic minds ever to grace the Christian pulpit." Commenting on Hull's *Harbingers of Hope,* Corts said, "Bill Hull has cultivated an indescribable capacity to juxtapose the Christian faith against the great ideas of modern man." Hull was awarded the Outstanding Educator Award by the Association of Southern Baptist Colleges and Schools. Hull holds a bachelor of arts degree from Samford University, a master of divinity degree and a doctor of philosophy degree from Southern Baptist Theological Seminary, and Advanced Studies degrees from the University of Göttingen, Germany, and Harvard University. He and his wife, Wylodine, have two adult children and two adult grandchildren.

Gerald L. Bray taught full-time at Beeson Divinity School in the areas of church history, historical theology, and Latin from 1993 to 2006. In 2006, he was named research professor and is currently engaged in writing and speaking on a variety of theological issues. A prolific author, Bray has published many scholarly articles and books, including *The Doctrine of God* in the Contours of Christian Theology Series (of which he is also the general editor) and *Biblical Interpretation: Past and Present*. He served as editor for *The Anglican Canons 1529–1947* and *Tudor Church Reform*, which contains the Henrician Canons of 1535 and the *Reformatio Legum Ecclesiasticarum*, and is also the editor of three volumes in the Ancient Christian Commentary Series. His most recent book, *Translating the Bible*, was published by the Latimer Trust in July 2010. Bray is a minister in the Church of England.

Lyle W. Dorsett has been the Billy Graham Professor of Evangelism at Beeson Divinity School since 2005 and teaches courses in evangelism and church history. He also serves as the pastor of Christ the King Anglican Church in Birmingham, Alabama (AMiA). He is the author of eighteen books, including several Christian biographies and three works on C. S. Lewis. His most recent book is *A Passion for God: The Spiritual Journey of A. W. Tozer*. He is married to Mary Hayes Dorsett, a deacon in AMiA. Together they founded Christ for Children International in Fresnillo, Zacatecas, Mexico. They have two children and four grandchildren.

Wayne Flynt is Professor Emeritus in the Auburn University Department of History. He has won numerous teaching awards and been a Distinguished University Professor for many years. His research focuses on Southern culture, Alabama politics, Southern religion, education reform, and poverty. He received his bachelor of arts degree from Howard College (now Samford University) in 1961, and both his master of science degree and doctorate from Florida State University. After teaching at Samford for eight years, he joined the faculty at Auburn University in 1977, where he remained for the rest of his academic career. He has written eleven books that focus largely on the historical, economic, and social fabric of Alabama, including two that were nominated for Pulitzer Prizes, *Poor But Proud: Alabama's Poor Whites* and *Alabama: A History of a Deep South State*, which he coauthored. Flynt's memoirs are published in *Keeping the Faith*. He is editor-in-chief of the online *Encyclopedia of Alabama*, a partnership of Auburn University and the Alabama Humanities Foundation.

Timothy George has been the dean of Beeson Divinity School since its inception in 1988. As founding dean, George has been instrumental in shaping its character and mission. He teaches church history and doctrine. He serves as executive editor for *Christianity Today*, the general editor of the *Reformation Commentary on*

Scripture, and is on the editorial advisory boards of *The Harvard Theological Review, Christian History,* and *Books & Culture.* He has also served on the board of directors of Lifeway Christian Resources of the Southern Baptist Convention. George has written more than twenty books and regularly contributes to scholarly journals. His book, *Theology of the Reformers,* has been translated into several languages and is used as a textbook in many schools and seminaries. His most recent books include: *Is the Father of Jesus the God of Muhammad?* and *The Mark of Jesus: Loving in a Way the World Can See* with John Woodbridge. He edited *J.I. Packer and the Evangelical Future,* co-edited *Our Sufficiency is of God: Essays on Preaching in Honor of Gardner C. Taylor,* and has been active in evangelical-Roman Catholic Church dialogue. An ordained Baptist minister, he has been the pastor of churches in Tennessee, Alabama, and Massachusetts. He and his wife, Denise, have two adult children.

Fisher Humphreys served as divinity professor at Samford University from 1990 until his retirement in 2008. In 2003 he was named the inaugural recipient of the Beeson Divinity School Teaching Award at Samford University. A specialist in the area of systematic theology, he is the author of more than ten books, including *Thinking About God,* which is widely used as an introduction to Christian theology. He has served as pastor of churches in Mississippi, Alabama, and Illinois.

Calvin Miller is a research professor and Distinguished Writer in Residence at Beeson Divinity School. Prior to his retirement from Beeson Divinity School in 2007, he was a professor of communication and ministry studies, and writer-in-residence at Southwestern Baptist

Theological Seminary. He previously served as pastor of Westside Baptist Church in Omaha, Nebraska. Miller is a poet, artist, novelist, and evangelist. He is the author of more than forty books and numerous articles on religion and preaching. His books include *The Empowered Communicator*, *Market-Place Preaching*, *Spirit, Word and Story*, *The Sermon Maker*, *O Shepherd, Where Art Thou?*; and *Preaching: The Art of Narrative Exposition*. He and his wife, Barbara, have two adult children.

J.I. Packer is a British-born Canadian Christian theologian in the low-church Anglican and Reformed Traditions. He is considered one of North America's most influential evangelicals. Following his ordination in the Anglican Church in 1958, Packer wrote his first book, called *Fundamentalism and the Word of God*, a critique of Christian fundamentalism. *Knowing God*, his most widely read book, was published fifteen years later in 1973. He worked to found the International Council on Biblical Inerrancy (ICBI). In 1979 he surprised the academic community by leaving his Anglican evangelical community to take a position at Regent College in Vancouver, British Columbia, where he currently serves as the Board of Governors' Professor of Theology. Packer is a prolific writer of more than fifty books and a frequent lecturer. He is a frequent contributor to and an executive editor of *Christianity Today*.

Eric Motley joined the Aspen Institute (Washington, D.C.) in 2007 as vice president and managing director of the Henry Crown Fellows Program. He currently serves as the executive director of the Aspen-Rockefeller Foundation's Commission to Reform the Federal Appointments Process. Motley formerly served as the director of the U.S. Department of State's Office of International Visitors within the bureau of Public Diplomacy. In 2003, he became Special Assistant to President George W. Bush for Presidential Personnel, where he managed the appointment process in the White House for over 1,200 presidentially-appointed advisory board and commission positions. He joined the White House staff as deputy associate director, Office of Presidential Personnel, in 2001 at the age of 27, immediately after receiving his doctorate. Motley earned his bachelor's degree in political science and philosophy from Samford University in 1996. As a Rotary International Ambassadorial Scholar at the University of St. Andrews in Scotland, he earned a master of letters in international relations and a doctorate in international relations as the John Steven Watson Scholar.

Roger Lovette is a Baptist minister who resides in Birmingham, Alabama. A native of Columbus, Georgia, Roger began his active ministry in 1961. He has held ministerial positions at churches in Kentucky, Virginia, South Carolina, Tennessee, and Alabama, and has served as an interim pastor for seven churches since his retirement. He has been a guest lecturer and preacher before many different audiences and writes frequently for journals on preaching. He is the author of five books, including *Journey Toward Joy: Directions from Philippians*, many articles, and a blog.

William A. Nunnelley is the director of media and public relations for Samford University and edits *Seasons*, the university's quarterly magazine. A widely acclaimed university publicist, he is an accredited member of the Public Relations Society of America (PRSA) and also holds membership in the Baptist Communicators Association (BCA) and Religion Communicators Council (RCC). *Seasons* has won awards from BCA, RCC, and the Council for the Advancement and Support of Education (CASE). Nunnelley holds a bachelor's degree in journalism and history and a master's degree in history from Samford. He has served in Samford's University Relations Department for more than four decades. He is the author of two books, *Bull Connor* and *Fred Shuttlesworth: Civil Rights Actionist*, a young reader's biography. He has written articles for *American Legacy, American History, World War II*, and *Georgia* magazines, and book reviews for the *Journal of Southern History*.